Aula

STIRLING
PUNISHMENTS

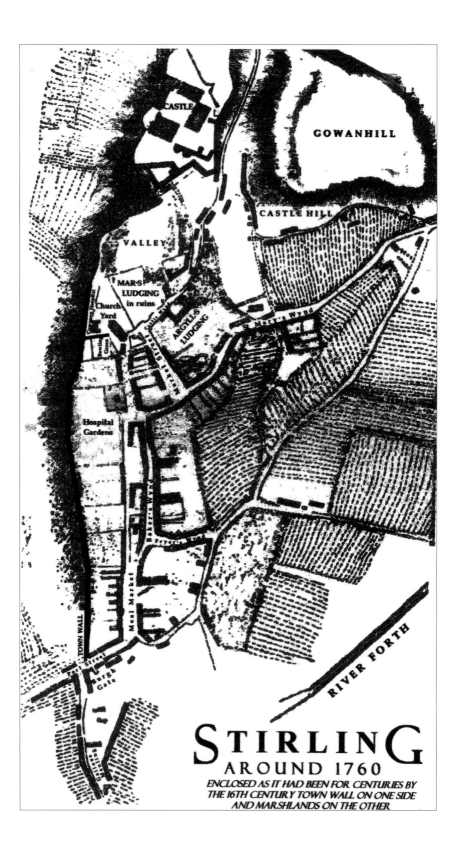

CASTLE

GOWANHILL

CASTLE HILL

VALLEY

MAR'S
LUDGING
in ruins

Church
Yard

ARGYLL'S
LUDGING

Hospital
Gardens

Meal Market

TOWN WALL

Burgh
Gate

RIVER FORTH

STIRLING
AROUND 1760
*ENCLOSED AS IT HAD BEEN FOR CENTURIES BY
THE 16TH CENTURY TOWN WALL ON ONE SIDE
AND MARSHLANDS ON THE OTHER*

Auld

STIRLING
PUNISHMENTS

David Kinnaird

The History Press

For Patricia Brannigan: having worked on the Stirling Ghost Walks
with me for ten years, she knows what punishment is all about.

First published 2011

The History Press
The Mill, Brimscombe Port
Stroud, Gloucestershire, GL5 2QG
www.thehistorypress.co.uk

© David Kinnaird, 2011

The right of David Kinnaird to be identified as the Author
of this work has been asserted in accordance with the
Copyrights, Designs and Patents Act 1988.

British Library Cataloguing in Publication Data.
A catalogue record for this book is available from the British Library.

ISBN 978 0 7524 6019 2

Typesetting and origination by The History Press
Printed in Great Britain

CONTENTS

ACKNOWLEDGEMENTS

The author would like to thank Tony Murray, Dr Elspeth King and her staff at the Smith Art Gallery and Museum, Stirling District Tourism and the staff of the old Town Jail, Alistair Campbell and the staff of the Tolbooth Theatre, Julia Sandford-Cooke, Patsy James of the Heritage Events Company, Rochelle MacDonald, Allan Goldie and Patricia Brannigan for their assistance and support during the writing of this text.

INTRODUCTION

Frae a' the bridewell cages an' blackholes,
And officers canes wi' halberd poles,
And frae the nine tail'd cat that opposes our souls,
Gude Lord deliver us.

(Traditional Scots grace)

Just before Christmas 2010, as I started preparing what I hoped would be the final draft of the book now in your hands, I was burgled. As if being robbed when one is in the process of producing a book on local crime and punishment wasn't replete with sufficient irony, I was – as my front door was splintered open, my lock shattered, and my sense of wellbeing sorely shaken – sitting, seasonally attired, in Santa's Grotto, telling tots tall tales of how a certain jolly, red-faced chap would soon be creeping into their homes and leaving little surprises for them. Ho, ho, ho! I was assuredly livid of cheek, but rather *less* than jolly, to discover that my PC and laptop had been trashed – and several months work lost.

This prompted two responses. The first was a sudden compulsion to cast off my long-cultivated *Guardian*-reading liberal sensibilities and fulminate furiously on plans for visiting upon my transgressors the self-same visceral punishments I'd been studying for so long. Secondly, with a deadline looming, was the more pressing concern of selectively reconstituting the salient points of what had been lost. Both reactions, the first borne of indignant ire, the latter of gut-wrenching panic, proved oddly productive. My anger – my righteous rage that the order of my home and my life had been set awry by an aberrant, anti-social invader who should (no, who *must*) be punished in order to set right the troubled microcosm of my world – provided me, I think, with a valuable insight into how the punishments instituted by our forefathers to protect their homes, their lives and their communities arose as safeguards against the chaos of the world at large.

My panic, similarly, helped me focus my gaze on those areas of history, and those particular punishments which inform us best about the mores and motives of those self-same citizens of Old Stirling. The Medieval era might well reveal a few gruesome, garish oddities, but the period between 1600 and 1900 saw the shaping of Stirling as we know it today – geographically and ideologically – and it was upon that era that I chose to linger longest.

As an actor and scriptwriter, I seem to have spent much of my professional life visiting Stirling's punitive past upon the heads of unsuspecting audiences. As a performer on the Stirling GhostWalk – my original dressing-room was the judge's robing room in the Tolbooth (the Burgh's preferred spelling) Jail   I helped to recreate several early sixteenth-century trials in the (late eighteenth-century) courtroom, and used the condemned cell (without ever knowing it was such) as a makeshift office for short-order script revisions. I'm still known chiefly in the town as a latter-day incarnation of the town's infamous last hangman, Jock Rankin, on the GhostWalks and within the Old Town Jail visitor attraction. I say 'last hangman', but…well, that point of local lore, like so many I was to touch upon while re-writing

The 'Last Hangman': Jock Rankin (author David Kinnaird) has become a familiar figure on the Stirling GhostWalk and at the Stirling Old Town Jail visitor attraction. (Picture courtesy of Stirling District Tourism)

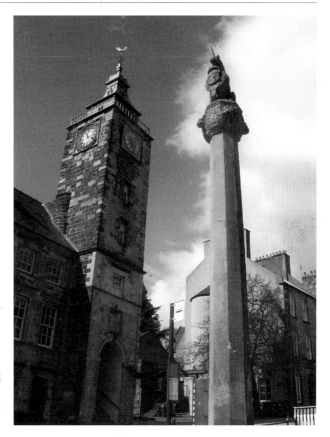

Crime and punishment: criminals tried at the Tolbooth would usually find justice served at the Mercat Cross in Market Street, now Broad Street. (Photo by David Kinnaird)

my manuscript, was a gobbet of received wisdom I'd find challenged by that pesky thing known as 'the facts'. As I discovered from my reaction to home-invasion, it's good to have one's preconceptions challenged – and I hope that you find the punitive parochial peculiarities of the Royal Burgh on the following pages as entertaining and informative as I did writing (and re-writing) them.

Incidentally, financial references until around 1700 are to Pounds Scots rather than Pounds Sterling (roughly a sixth of the value). References to monarchs following the 1606 Union of Crowns note the Scots and English ranking – James the Sixth of Scotland and First of England being, accordingly, James VII

Before we continue, a few words about Stirling – the 'place of strife', as the odd Scots/Gaelic etymology of the name (variously *Sruighlea*, *Strivelin* or *Stirlin*) suggests. A she-wolf rests, recumbent on the coat of arms decorating the entrance to the courtroom of the Tolbooth, celebrating the feared and fabled beast whose baleful howls alerted seventh-century Northumbrian settlers upon the Castle Crag to Viking onslaught in the dead of night. It was one of the principal strongholds of Scots monarchy from the time of David I, who granted Stirling its celebrated status as a Royal Burgh in 1130, and it remained a favoured seat of the Royal House of Stuart – who took their name from Walter Stewart, High Steward of Scotland, husband to Robert Bruce's daughter, Margaret, and father to the first of that famous line, Robert II. Next to the coursing flood of the River Forth, the walled community of the Castle Rock was the 'Key to Scotland', dividing Highland from Lowland – the stronghold of all who would hold fast to the nation since Agricola clashed with Calgacus at *Mons Graupius*. Falling from courtly favour after the 1603 Union of Crowns, it remained a hub of Caledonian commerce and light industry, with a busy port. It boasts a university, opened in 1967, and a population of around 45,000. Smaller than many of the country's larger towns, it became Scotland's newest city in 2002, as part of Queen Elizabeth II's Golden Jubilee celebrations.

David Kinnaird, 2011

1

EARLY PLACES OF PUNISHMENT

The Heading Hill

Occupying a small plateau to the north-east of Stirling Castle, a lesser mound of the greater Gowanhill, lies Mote Hill – known more commonly to Stirling residents as 'The Heading Hill'. Easily accessible from the sweep of the Back Walk, the line of the defensive Medieval Burgh Wall, it is thought to contain the vestigial remnants of a Pictish hill fort, though the last visible relics of that ancient structure, a low wall described by surveyors in 1794 (at which time it was known as 'Murdoch's Hill'), have long since vanished – probably plundered, like so many local ruins, for building materials. If it was a fort or settlement, serving the needs of an early community on the Castle Rock, then the name is fitting, such places (*mons placeti*, or statute hills) being used for moots – public gatherings, proclamations and punishments.

The hill, today, is dominated by two captured Napoleonic cannon, pointing out over the Stirling Bridge and Abbey Craig – sites significant in William Wallace's victory over the occupying English Army, on 11 September 1297 – and by the conical iron covering of the ancient Beheading Stone.

The origins of the stone are unknown, though its close proximity to the castle and its visibility from the town seems to confirm the site's appropriateness for courtly punishment: elevated and apart from the town, but, like the fortress in whose shadow it rests, commanding the attention of all. Beheading was reserved for those guilty of High Treason (the attendant punishments of 'drawing' and 'quartering' being only selectively enacted in Scottish ritual), and applied, therefore, to principally aristocratic felons, such as Murdoch Stewart, Duke of Albany. Grandson of Robert II, Stewart had ruled as Governor of Scotland during the eighteen-year English imprisonment of James I, insinuating his kin into positions of power and authority. When James' £40,000 ransom was finally paid he returned to his homeland, launching pre-emptive attacks on those noble families whom he felt to pose a threat to his newfound authority. Foremost

The Beheading Stone: Mote Hill, a place of punishment since the Iron Age, sits in the shadow of Stirling Castle. (Photo by David Kinnaird)

amongst these were the Albany Stewarts. Condemned for his mismanagement of the kingdom, the former Governor was beheaded along with his sons Walter and Alisdair, and his father-in-law, Donnchadh of Lennox, effectively hobbling the ambitions of the dynasty. His only surviving heir, 'James the Fat', fled to Antrim, Ireland, where he died in 1429.

An unpopular King, having diverted funds raised for the liberation of other ransomed Scots nobles into self-aggrandizing constructions, such as his new palace at Linlithgow, he quickly detained or executed many other rivals, amongst them Alexander, Lord of the Isles, Archibald Douglas and George, Earl of March. James was eventually murdered at Perth, on 20 February 1437, during an unsuccessful coup by another cousin, Walter Stewart, Earl of Atholl. No doubt inspired by his bloody example, James' English bride, Queen Joan Beaufort, ordered the execution of the instrument of Walter's ambition, Robert Graham, later that same year. After a three-day public exhibition of scourging, branding – a heated coronet searing the words 'King of Traytors' upon his brow – crucifixion, gradual dismemberment (his hands and feet cut off and cauterized) and partial strangulation, he was beheaded. He is recalled in the old verse:

> Robert Graham
> Who slew our King,
> God give him shame.

Lesser punishments almost certainly occurred upon Mote Hill, though records of these do not survive. Justice would increasingly be enforced in other public places, quickly establishing themselves within the Burgh: at the Tron or Mercat Cross, with the construction of the new Tolbooth at the end of the fifteenth-century, entrenching a new oligarchical form of burgh government; and at the Barras Yett.

The Beheading Stone was *not* employed during the most infamous executions for treason in Stirling's history, those of the Radical Weavers John Baird and Andrew Hardie, in 1822. Long thought lost, it was rediscovered sunken into the sod near the Old Stirling Bridge in 1887, where it had been used by several generations of local butchers for de-horning sheep carcasses. Rescued by the Stirling Natural History and Archaeology Society, it was restored to its original home upon the Mote Hill the following year.

The Burgh Wall

The line of the Back Walk, a scenic pathway completed to a plan by William Edmonston of Cambus Wallace in 1791, has provided visitors to the Burgh with panoramic views of the Old Town and surrounding countryside for generations – quickly proving itself to be one of the area's first tourist attractions. Towering ominously over this pretty pathway stand the finest surviving remains of a medieval town wall in Scotland, whose line it follows from Dumbarton Road, in the heart of the contemporary city, to the castle itself. The wall, completed in 1547 with monies raised by the Burgesses and nobility of the Burgh, including Mary de Guise, mother of the infant Mary, Queen of Scots, and widow of James V, who ordered its construction, 'to expend upoun the strengthing and bigging of the walls of the toune at this present peralus tyme of neid, for resisting our auld innimeis of Ingland' – protected both town and Crown from the ambitions of England's King Henry VIII, who sought to remove the young Queen from Stirling Castle, and, through betrothal to his own sickly heir, Edward (later, Edward VI), force a union of the two nations. The new defences were erected just in time to protect the communities of the Castle Rock from the worst devastations of what Sir Walter Scott would later term the 'Rough Wooing'. English forces reached the town only a few weeks after completion, in September 1547.

The Burgh Wall: the sixteenth-century defensive wall raised by Mary de Guise to fend off the English, during the 'Rough Wooing', shaped Stirling's destiny for centuries to come. (Photo by David Kinnaird)

To the north marshland made the town virtually unassailable. The Town Wall, therefore, was no mere defensive barrier, it was the key to understanding how Stirling *worked* as a unique social and political organism, and how it related to the outside world – particularly where issues of crime, punishment and the administration of justice are concerned – for the next three centuries.

The Gallows Mauling

There was, almost certainly, a much earlier wall: albeit a simple elevated earth rampart or wooden palisade. Records for 1522 mention the 'Barras Yett' – or Burgh Gate – and a 'burrows port' is referred to as early as 1477, though chroniclers carelessly neglect to state what the gate in question was *attached* to. There were, of course, several lesser gates – the Brig Port, near Stirling Bridge and the New Port, from which modern Port Street takes its name – but the

The Barras Yett: The site of this ancient portal to the Royal Burgh can be still be found in the heart of the modern city, at the intersection of Port Street. and Dumbarton Road. (Photo by David Kinnaird)

broader Barras Yett strictly controlled access and egress to and from the town. It was the portal through which vagrants and vagabonds would be forbidden access, and from which those who had earned the enmity of the Burgh Court would be forever banished. Within sight of the gate – recalled by a simple pavement plaque at the modern intersection of Dumbarton Road and Port Street – stands the Victorian Black Boy fountain, dedicated to the staggering 30 per cent of Stirling's population who perished from the plague during its 'visitation' of 1369. Despite its grim associations, this monument is a long-established place of public celebration. Locals gathered beneath it on VJ-Day, on 14 August 1945, when the *Stirling Journal* reported that 'The Black Boy fountain was brilliantly lighted... Gaily coloured lights hung from the trees and the sight was one resembling fairyland.' Clamorous gatherings on this spot had long been common, of course – but beneath a rather less festive bough. This was the original site of the Gallows Mauling (or Mailing) – the location of the public gibbet, or 'gallows tree', described by Victorian historian William Drysdale in *Old Faces, Old Places and Old Stories of Stirling* (1899) as:

The Gallows Mauling: the Black Boy fountain, a pretty Victorian monument to fourteenth-century plague victims, marks the site where the town gallows was once erected. (Photo by David Kinnaird)

A wooden beam fixed in a large stone, with a crossbar at its top, and a number of hooks fixed thereon. The unfortunates had to ascend one ladder, and the hangman another, and, after adjusting the rope, he pushed the culprits off to their fate, and then removed his ladder.

Executions occurred here until at least 16 May 1788, when forger John Smart was marched from the Tolbooth jail, through the Hangman's Entry, along the line of the Town Wall and through the archway of the Barras Yett – symbolically expelled from the body and life of the town before he met his dismal end on the public gib. Future executions would occur in Market Street (now Broad Street), in the heart of the Old Town, by which time the ancient defences were finally being dismantled, allowing expansion over and beyond the old Burgh boundaries.

The Thieves' Hole

A more palpable (and accessible) reminder of past punishment within the walled Burgh is to be found beneath the Port Street entrance to the modern Thistles shopping centre. A winding spiral staircase leads visitors into The Bastion, a sixteenth-century guard-room, complete with *Thieves' Pot*, a subterranean bottle-dungeon into which nocturnal drunkards and mischief makers might be thrown by the Town Guard and detained overnight until they could be transferred to the cells of the Tolbooth. Believed to be part of Mary de Guise's 1547 fortification of the Town Wall, and similar to the somewhat larger defensive tower of the Gunpowder Battery still visible on the ruined Town Wall, it may actually pre-date that structure, and was still in use at the end of the seventeenth-century, when Treasurer's records note the sum of two shillings paid 'for oyle to the irones in the thieves holl quen the Liddells [a family of notorious roister-doisters] wes put there.'

The Last Bastion: beneath the modern Thistles shopping centre lie the restored remains of a sixteenth-century defensive tower and lock-up. (Photo by David Kinnaird, courtesy of the Thistles shopping centre)

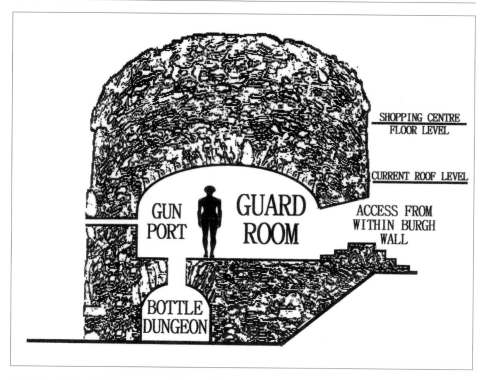

SHOPPING CENTRE
FLOOR LEVEL

CURRENT ROOF LEVEL

GUN
PORT

GUARD
ROOM

ACCESS FROM
WITHIN BURGH
WALL

BOTTLE
DUNGEON

The Thieve's Pot: The Bastion served as a holding-cell for troublemakers within the town, and as a defence against attack from outside. (Illustration by David Kinnaird)

Decals and dioramas explain the part the structure played in the exercise of local justice and defence, displayed alongside the regalia of the Town Officers and the pug-faced figure of Justice which once adorned the entrance to the medieval Tolbooth, which preceded the current building. As we will see in subsequent chapters, in consideration of the Tron, Mercat Cross and other places of common punishment within the developing Royal Burgh between 1600 and 1850, Stirling's punitive past is rarely far from the surface of the modern town.

2

THE BURGH

The Tolbooth

Just as the castle dominates the Stirling skyline, a constant reminder of the power and majesty of the Stuart kings who called it home, the pavilioned Dutch clock-tower of the Tolbooth looms imposingly over the homes and businesses of the Old Town, in stern remembrance of the more immediate authority that buildings on this spot have exorcised over the local population for half a millennium. From the earliest days of the Royal Burgh the administration of local affairs was centred here. The first such building to occupy the current site in Broad Street was a largely wooden construction, erected in 1472. A rather more substantial stone structure appeared in 1575-76. Consisting of a courtroom and cells, a council chamber, an office where local tolls and taxes could be paid, a steeple and vaults, virtually nothing remains of either of these early edifices, though a 'hol beneth the steeple' still used as a storeroom, and recorded as having being in use immediately prior to an even more extensive rebuilding between 1703 and 1705 – to designs drawn up by Sir William Bruce of Kinross, described by Defoe as the 'Christopher Wren of North Britain' – may be the last remnant of these original structures. In 1785 Gideon Gray, also responsible for the local Grammar School (now the Portcullis Hotel) and Wingate's Inn (currently the Golden Lion Hotel), seamlessly extended Bruce's Broad Street frontage – his work described in Burgh records as 'an extension of the Town House, prison and Clerk's Office'. A final stage of development – at a cost of £1,583 10s 8d – followed between 1808 and 1810, with the addition of a new courtroom, cells and the prison block looking onto St John Street – designed by Edinburgh architect Richard Creighton. One significant feature of Creighton's courtroom was the provision of public seating; most courts having previously met in private within various small rooms within the Town House, and public participation in proceedings actively discouraged.

Its functions gradually superseded by the construction of the current Municipal Buildings, Sheriff Court and Old Town Jail, the Tolbooth manages, still, to remain

The Tolbooth: William Bruce's majestic eighteenth-century clock-tower dominates the modern Old Town, as other buildings on this site have for almost a millennium. (Photo by David Kinnaird)

A grim memento: one of the cell doors from Gideon Gray's 1785 cell-block adorns a stairwell wall in the modern theatre.

at the heart of local life, having seen service as a workhouse, an army recruiting post, a restaurant, tourist development offices and, most recently, a theatre and arts centre. Many of the features of Bruce, Gray and Creighton's structures were restored between 2000 and 2001, during renovations by conservation architects Simpson and Brown.

The Tolbooth was not a prison as we would understand the term today. It was the dedicated seat of burgh government: a combined office of public record, civil administration and justice. Cells were required under renewed terms which confirmed the self-governing powers of the Royal Burghs, in 1469, but prisoners were rarely sentenced to set periods of penal servitude within its walls. Until the late eighteenth-century, custodial sentences, save for those assigned to the hard labour of the Workhouse, or House of Correction, were virtually unheard of – as was the notion that incarceration might in some way reform the characters of criminals. Jails were essentially little more than holding areas for those pending trial or, if already sentenced, awaiting the 'pleasure of the court' – whether that be the payment of fines, whipping, branding, banishment or execution. Given the transient nature of prison populations, there was seen as being little point in maintaining the cells in good order. As the Victorian era of improvement and innovation began to dawn, the Tolbooth continued as it had for two centuries or more: even the most modern parts of the building showing no reflection of changing ideas of prison construction The problems were fundamental, as one Circuit Court Judge, cited in John G. Harrison's paper 'The Stirling Tollbooth: The Building and its People, 1472-1847' (1989), observed:

> In the prison of Stirling there is, and can be, no classification of prisoners…In this prison the tried and the untried must necessarily be huddled together. The poor girl taken up for the first time, probably for some paltry offence, or for concealment of pregnancy, is placed in the company of hardened criminals, the thief by habit of repute. What can be the result of such things but contamination to the mind, ruin to the character in this world, and, it may be, perdition in the world to come?

'No doubt there were at one time, and in some places,' the Judge seethes, 'jails even more wretched…but there has been no jail to my knowledge in which such a fearful state of things existed as has been the case in the prison of Stirling.' Birmingham-born Frederick Hill, a passionate Reformer and acolyte of Elizabeth Fry, would soon be created first Inspector of Prisons for Scotland, and was similarly outraged by his first visit to the jail, in 1836. He complained that '[the] masonry… is so bad that holes can easily be made through the walls; so that even security, the most evident of all requisites in a prison, has not been adequately cared for,' and that no inmate could be safely set to work 'lest he should employ his tools in making his way through the frail tenement in which he was confined.'

Hidden stairway: rediscovered during renovations, this stairwell was thought to link the cells and courtroom; it actually provided jury access to the court. (Photo by David Kinnaird)

Escapes from the prison throughout the previous two centuries had been a constant source of embarrassment, and almost every page in the Treasurer's records for the latter half of the eighteenth century details monies paid for the correction of damage sustained through criminals' egressive efforts. Sometimes very little effort was required. On 11 March 1839, Daniel Martin and William Anderson simply walked out of the front door, assisted by turnkey Andrew Towers. Structural problems were nothing new: the construction of Bruce's building being largely the result of legal action brought against the Council by neighbours, fearful that its tottering medieval predecessor might collapse and crush their own properties.

Those liberated from the Tolbooth did not always escape by their own efforts. In a dispute over paternity, recorded in the nearby Parish of Logie in 1698, Angus Livingstone confessed freely to being the father of a child delivered of Isobel Hatton some years earlier. Asked why he had not honoured his paternal obligations until that time, he confessed that he was 'taken to be a soldier' from the Stirling Tolbooth. Each parish was obliged, under law, to provide men to serve in the forces – or yield to the Crown cash in lieu. Often vagrants and undesirables, detained in town jails for petty offences, would be chosen for such service, but it was not unknown for

Press Gangs, eager to fill their quotas, to take matters into their own hands, bribe jailors or simply force entry to provincial cells. In Stirling their job would have been made easier, both by the poor condition of the building, and because the cells were left unattended at night, the jailor locking the doors and leaving inmates to their own devices (still the case in the 1830s, when Hill complained that 'the Keeper does not reside on the spot'). Enforced recruitment of able-bodied men was a perennial problem for poorer communities, who might be deprived of essential labour: their families left without breadwinners as Press Gangs tricked, taunted or cruelly coerced men to 'Take the King's Shilling'.

In 1702, Stirling's Burgh Court heard several cases brought against local women who had assaulted a Press Gang, driving them off the streets under a hail of abuse, cobble-stones and horse muck. One garrulous Gudewife, Mary Weir, denied having participated in the affray, but swore that 'if she had heard of it sooner, she would have'. Charges were dropped, and the next day a proclamation was made at the market, assuring citizens that the Provost and Bailies would support any honest citizen seized by the Press Gangs by petitioning the Privy Council on their behalf. Such an appeal, shortly afterwards, ensured the liberation of three Cambuskenneth weavers – 'douce, sober, honest, married *men*' – who had been cruelly separated from their families in this manner.

Market Street: public punishments required a public venue. Where better than the weekly market? (Image reproduced by kind permission of the Stirling Smith Art Gallery and Museum)

BROKE PRISON.

FIFTEEN GUINEAS REWARD.

WHEREAS betwixt the hours of Seven and Eight o'Clock last night, being the 11th day of March instant, DANIEL MARTIN, *alias* ROBERT BAIN, and WILLIAM ANDERSON, *alias* JAS. WILSON, *alias* JAMES M'NEILL, Criminal Prisoners in the Jail of Stirling, made their Escape therefrom, with the assistance of ANDREW TOWERS, one of the Turnkeys, who has absconded, the Magistrates of Stirling do hereby offer

A REWARD OF FIVE GUINEAS
for the apprehension and committal to any of her Majesty's Goals, within one Month from this date, of each of the said Daniel Martin, and William Anderson, and Andrew Towers; which Rewards shall be paid by ROBERT SCONCE, Procurator Fiscal of the Burgh of Stirling.

Daniel Martin, *alias* Robert Bain, is a native of Glasgow, 18 years of age, and a Tailor to trade, at which he worked for some time at Stenhousemuir and Falkirk. He is 5 feet 10½ inches in height, pale complexion, blue eyes, and brown hair. He had on when he went away a blue pea jacket with a brown fur collar, a black and white check vest, brown and white striped trowsers, laced boots, and a black hat.

William Anderson, *alias* James Wilson, *alias* James M'Neill, is a native of Ayr, about 21 years of age, and a Millwright to trade. He is 5 feet 2½ inches in height, dark complexion, grey eyes, and dark hair. He had on, when he made his escape, a brown jacket, black vest, brown striped trowsers, frieze hunting cap, and laced boots.

Andrew Towers is a native of Stirling, 22 years of age, about 5 feet 8 inches high, fair complexion and blue eyes, and is supposed to have had on, when he went off, a blue pea jacket, striped vest, dark brown striped trowsers, and a blue bonnet.

COUNCIL CHAMBERS,
Stirling, 12th March, 1839.

Prison break: escapes from the Tolbooth were all too frequent, much to the embarrassment of the Bailies. (Item from the Dundee *Courier*, Author's collection)

To Frederick Hill the very location of the jailhouse, immediately adjacent to the busy marketplace, was a problem. 'The prison is placed in so public a situation that it would be impossible to prevent communication from without,' he wrote despairingly, 'an object…which does not appear to have entered the heads of those that made the place'. On this point, Hill was quite wrong. Prisoners, save for those rare few who were granted special dispensation (usually on account of their impending execution), or who had sufficient funds to buy food, were not normally provided with sustenance during their confinement, and were required to beg for food through the ground-level cell windows. This, in itself, provided entertainment for visitors on Market Day, and numerous accounts appear of locals lining up to view 'vagrants, now held in our Tollbooth'. Amongst their number may have been the 'Ploughman Poet', Robert Burns, who was mobbed by ardent fans near the

Tolbooth when he visited the town in 1787. Burns was fortunate that his famously seditious *Lines on Stirling*, scratched on a window pane of Wingate's Inn with an engravers' pencil – and which described the ruling Hanoverian dynasty as 'an idiot race, to honour lost' – didn't serve to make his acquaintance with the building rather more intimate.

Hill's most scathing criticisms were reserved for the 'means of separation' of prisoners. 'All the females, of which there are sometimes twelve or fifteen at one time, are huddled together in the same room,' he wrote, and 'conversation can readily be kept up between the females and the males.' The young Reformer was outraged to relate that 'about twelve months ago one of the females bored a hole through the wall into the adjoining males' cell.' Tales concerning the questionable uses to which that hole was subsequently put have long been part of local lore. Frederick would have been more outraged had he visited those same cells only a few decades earlier. Although the segregation of male and female prisoners was an obligation of the Court, it was not always honoured. Men, women and children as young as six years of age were commonly held together. The only real segregation was reserved for religious or political dissenters – such as Duncan McPhie of Lochaber, held here in May 1760, 'suspected of being a vagrant person and concerned in enticing some of the Highland battalion in the town to desert' – who, it was feared, might agitate other inmates.

Of the ten cells available, only two were reserved, by 1844 – by which time Hill would have been relieved to know that two male and two female officers were on duty, even at night – for female prisoners. In September of that year, one cell was solely occupied by a violent 'female lunatic'. With three prisoners 'lying in bed sick', separated from the general population, that left an astonishing twenty-four prisoners huddled together in one cell only slightly larger than a modern single bedroom. Overcrowded and unsanitary – one local physician, Dr Robert Forrest of Spittall Street, bewailed the fact that 'more died there of the dirt than ever did by the hangman's hemp' – the Tolbooth was condemned by the Inspector of Prisons as 'the worst jail in Britain', in an official report published in 1842. Though reforms and improvements were soon to come, it would yet have a part to play in the judicial and criminal life of the town.

First Prison Inspector: Reformer Frederick Hill, who condemned the Tolbooth as the 'worst jail in Britain'. (Sketch by David Kinnaird, based upon original photographs)

(COPY.)—RETURN from the Keeper of the Prison of Stirling of the number of Cells and Prisoners in Stirling Prison, on the 1st of the Months undermentioned.													
Dates.	Number of cells for confinement during the night.			Number of prisoners at the dates specified.			Greatest & least number confined together in the same cell or room.				Whether the convicted are kept separate from the unconvicted.	Number of officers who sleep in the prison.	
							Greatest		Least.				
	Males.	Females.	Total.	Males.	Females.	Total.	Males.	Females.	Males.	Females.		Males.	Females.
1844 May 1	8	2	10	47	13	60	11	9	2	4			
June 1				48	14	62	13	10	2	4			
July 1				46	19	65	10	16	2	2	No.	2	2
Aug. 1				50	26	76	8	20	2	6			
Sept. 1				37	27	64	9	24	2	3			

SEPT. 24.—IN JAIL THIS DAY.

	Males.	Females.	Total.
Untried,............	10	6	16
Convicted, ...	25	22	47
Civil prisoners,...	4	0	4
			67

Since 1st of June the number of Stirlingshire prisoners has run from 56 the lowest number, to 70 the highest.

The Clackmannanshire prisoners were in addition to these numbers, but they were removed finally on the 13th of August.

There are only two rooms for females, one is, at present, occupied exclusively by a female lunatic, but whose state of mind is to be investigated, as directed by the Statute, on Monday. Three of the female prisoners are lying in bed sick.

Stirling's shame: overcrowded and unsanitary, the Tolbooth was deemed 'the worst prison in Britain'. One visiting Judge published the Keeper's records in a number of national newspapers. (Item from the *Glasgow Herald*, Author's collection)

The Bailies – Brothers and Strangers

To considering the Bailies – the Magistrates of Stirling who presided within the Tolbooth from the fifteenth until the early nineteenth-centuries, we must first understand a little of the class and culture from which they emerged.

From King David I's Charter of 1130, by which Stirling was created a Royal Burgh, those who wished to participate in the government of their community were required to pay the price of their ambition – as indicated in a later edict, issued by Alexander II, in 1226, wherein the King commanded, 'that those who dwell within our burgh of Stirling and who wish to take part with our Burgesses at the market shall take part with them in contributing to our aids.'

A modest payment allowed a man to become a manufacturer, and a larger sum gain him membership of one of the Seven Incorporated Trades – hammermen (blacksmiths), baxters (bakers), wrights and coopers (carpenters and barrel-makers), tailors, shoemakers, weavers and fleshers (butchers). A larger toll might allow him to become a merchant, and seek entry to the Guildry. Guild members would routinely outnumber members of the Crafts or Incorporations on Council, until the start of the nineteenth century, by a ratio of two to one. Thus monopolies on all matters relating to trade were established, both within Stirling's own markets and in its commercial dealing with other towns. These Burgesses (from the French *bourgeois*), as those encouraged by Royal decree in 'contributing to our aids' were known, were not merely traders: doctors, lawyers, bankers, barbers, schoolteachers (a 'peri-wig maker' is included in their ranks in the 1750s) and any other property-owning citizen with the inclination and *capital* – applicants had to demonstrate substantial liquid assets as evidence of suitability to trade – to participate in government could seek Guildry membership. This in turn would protect their commercial privileges, and through periodic payment to the Crown, preserve the Burgh's provisional right to self-government. These protections, of course, did not extent to those deemed to participate in 'inconsiderable trade', women or common citizens, who lacked the wealth to seek membership of such prestigious associations. While Burgesses referred to one another as 'neighbours' and 'brothers', in official documents, the general population were termed as 'strangers' or 'unfreemen and women'. As John G. Harrison observes in the paper 'The World of John Cowane' (1989), a study of the life and times of Stirling's most famous seventeenth-century burgess and benefactor, 'in the overall control of public life their interests were largely ignored...Stirling should be seen as a community of the privileged, co-operating with other similar communities.'

As Guild membership was a heritable privilege, passed on to their heirs at little or no additional cost, it should be no surprise that this urban elite was self-perpetuating: the same names – Cowane, Spittal, Jaffrey, Robertson and Burd, to name but a few – occupy key positions within the Guild and the Council throughout the sixteenth,

Leaving their mark: the distinctive 'reverse-four' mark of Stirling's Guildry can still be seen on many headstones in the Holy Rude kirkyard. (Photo by David Kinnaird)

seventeenth and eighteenth centuries. The Guildry's grip on parochial policy and purse-strings begins to slip only when Stirling ceases to be an important trading town during the early nineteenth century, and laws were changed – the Royal Burghs Act (1833) depriving Guildry of their two-third Council majority.

There were usually between twenty-one and twenty-four members of the Council, representing the various burgess communities – each new administration elected by the previous one, from lists supplied by the Incorporations and Guildry. Rules requiring rotation were in place from the sixteenth century, in order to prevent ambitious individuals from entrenching self-serving power-bases, but these were generally ignored. Until the early seventeenth century even the most prestigious public office, that of Provost, was popularly held to be in the political gift of the Earls of Mar. Local landowner John Murray of Touchadam, for example, occupied the office virtually uninterrupted from 1590 until 1609. While the Provost was the ceremonial and public face of the Burgh, the role of *Preses* – presiding over everyday administration of town affairs – was largely taken by the Dean of Guild, further reinforcing links between the commercial, political and administrative life of the community. Guild dominance of Council often led to tension with the Trades. During one such dispute, in 1613, John Paterson assaulted Provost Duncan Paterson. Intent on making a 'hole-in-one' with the curious combination of a dagger and a golf club, he was fined £40, paraded at the Mercat Cross, and demanded to 'openly crave God, the King's Majesty, the said Provost and all the magistrates of this burgh's, forgiveness for his offence' – then made to pay a further £100 bond against his future good conduct. Where the preservation of precious monopolies were concerned, the Guildry-dominated Council did not just enforce the law, they *were* the law.

A better illustration is perhaps provided by the case of the Cudbert brothers. In the early 1690s, national legislation sought to extend to rural traders rights previously only enjoyed by Guildry within the Royal Burghs. The Cudbert family sought to take advantage of this move, and began a trade in goat skins which they had not themselves manufactured – this still being a monopoly enjoyed by the *Brothers*. In the summer of 1692, travelling from Stirling with two packs of skins, with the intention of selling his wares in Edinburgh, Thomas Cudbert was stopped by the Dean of Guild and beaten roughly with a staff. Thomas successfully sued the Dean for assault, but his confiscated skins were returned only after many months, and with the oath that he would never repeat his 'offence'. Clearly irked by his unfair treatment, Cudbert seemed to take delight over the coming years in challenging the authority of the Guildry, and, in turn, the Council itself. After setting up a shop in the town which sold a variety of goods still seen as the exclusive preserve of the burgesses, he was imprisoned in the Tolbooth, on the order of the Provost himself – acting as chief magistrate, but with the interests of his Guild brethren foremost in his mind. Liberated on the order of the Court of Session, Thomas put forward

Norrie's house: home of seventeenth-century Town Clerk, James Norrie. With the Bailies having very little knowledge of judicial process, the Clerk often served to guide them in matters of due process. (Photo by David Kinnaird)

a passionate and convincing defence: since trading rights had been extended to rural traders, surely it was absurd to suggest that these privileges did not apply to urban artisans like himself, trading within the Royal Burghs. After many months, incurring great expense for the family – chiefly because they were not permitted to trade until a ruling was forthcoming – the Court of Session found in favour of the Stirling Provost and Bailies. The ancient charters of the Burghs must be honoured: if he wished to do business reserved for the *Brothers*, Thomas must seek entry to the Guild, or else cease trade forthwith. A decade later Thomas' redoubtable spouse, Bessie Murris, challenged the Bailies ruling that only merchants of the Incorporation of Weavers (whom she described as 'a pack of brozie [brazen] faced rascals') had the right to buy and sell wool in the town – by buying up all the wool in Stirling and for six miles around. She was fined, threatened with imprisonment, and forced to give an undertaking not to repeat her offence. Such a sustained and systematic defiance of the much-abused authority of burgess-Bailies was rare, and cost the Cudberts dearly, time and time again.

And thus we come to the Bailies – the magistrates and arbiters of law. These were four in number – originally little more than tax collectors within the Medieval

Burgh, though nothing of this original function remained by the start of the seventeenth century. These were burgesses-councillors, elected each September, ostensibly by the retiring and incumbent councils combined, though even here political patronage and graft was not uncommon. Harrison reports the umbrage taken by one new Provost during a fleeting period of reform, disappointed that he had not 'have, in manner, the naming of the Council'. Aside from sitting in judgement over all crimes, misdemeanours and disputes brought before the courts, each Bailie had a specific responsibility for a particular Quarter of the town, and played a major part in town planning and 'the public weil' (wellbeing) within his designated area.

The upper ranks of the Guildry and the senior officers of the Council being drawn from the same burgess stock, it is unsurprising that the aims and interests of the traders and the town were indistinguishable. To modern eyes this, of course, seems astonishingly self-serving. Even when efforts were made, nationally, to curtail the political influence of prominent statesmen such as the Earls of Mar, and gentlemen Provosts were supplanted by a succession of trading Merchants in the mid-seventeenth century, the principal objective of the Council remained the maintenance of monopolies and preservation of privilege for the elite to which they belonged – who, it is estimated (and including their families and dependants), represented less than 20 per cent of the Burgh population. The equation between property and the exercise of government is the single most common feature of municipalities within northern Europe from Medieval times. Their self-interest will be a key factor in considering the means and manner of punishment to be discussed later.

Their us-and-them attitude is ably illustrated by the experience of Jonet Kilbowie, who kept a tavern in Bow Street – currently occupied by the Darnley Coffee House and known to locals as Darnley's House, on account of the popular belief that it was once a popular haunt of Henry, Lord Darnley, short-lived second husband to Mary, Queen of Scots (it clearly wasn't, not having been built until more than half a century after his murder at Kirk o' Field, on 10 February 1567). R.S. Fleming, in *The Old Ludgings of Stirling* (1897), tells of a gathering there, in August 1651, whereby the Council and Bailies elected to yield to the forces of the General Monck, at which they ran up a quite remarkable bar bill of £10 11s 4d for wines and spirits. Six months later poor Mistress Kilbowie was still seeking settlement of their account. In dealing with a woman and a 'stranger' (though born and bred within the Burgh), the Councillors clearly saw no need for haste in settlement of their tab. Had someone defaulted in their payment to a *Brother* they would have been promptly fined by the Bailies. For labouring the issue of their debt, Kilbowie was herself punished – fined for selling 'ower pricet ale'.

'The Black Bond'

The conditions for corruption within such an insular system being so glaringly apparent, it comes as some surprise to note the apparent shock manifest by many in the local population when conspicuous graft was brought to their attention – though this may, of course, simply signify the disdain of the urban elite at having their dirty laundry flaunted freely in public. In 1695 an oath was introduced for Council members, obliging them to:

> take no lease of any part of public property, nor to purchase any part of it; neither to receive gratification out of the public funds, under pretence of a reward for their trouble in going about the affairs of the borough, or the hospitals founded in it.

This was the result of a ruling by the Court of Sessions, in Edinburgh, which found that former Provost Robert Russell and his relations had 'embezzled the common good' and 'by contrivance and combination continued themselves in the magistracy of the burgh' during the preceding three decades.

A greater scandal was to come. In 1773 a letter, written around 1771 – and quickly earning itself the suitably melodramatic appellation of *The Black Bond* – was published. Written by Bailies James Burd and Henry Jaffrey and Provost James Alexander the letter detailed, in staggeringly unsubtle manner, the terms of a pact between the three to 'secure to ourselves the total management of the Burgh during our lives…for the benefit of Us and our friends.' They stated their clear intent to 'weaken the interest' of fellow councillor and rival Nicol Bryce, 'and by degrees to exclude him and his friends from the council altogether'. Those seeking election to prominent positions paid for the privilege – such as Town Clerk John McGibbon, 'elected' in 1766, who arranged (for the sum of £25, yearly, to be deducted by the conspirators from his salary) that his son should be appointed his assistant and successor. This scheme is more insidious than it seems. Since only Councillors were legally entitled to vote in parliamentary elections the 'Black Bondsmen' could sell their votes, and those of others in their thrall. The instigator of the plot was not, as one might assume, the Provost Alexander, described by one observer as being no natural leader of men, being 'of a very facile disposition', and whose principal claims to fame – aside from corruption – were his possession of a particularly foul-mouthed cockatoo and his part in founding The Stirling Banking Company (his double-share in which quickly allowed him to buy out his partners, amassing a considerable fortune in the process). The scheme was the work of the rather more formidable Bailie Burd, who looms from contemporary accounts like a gloriously grotesque caricature of pantomime villainy. 'A man more feared than respected', Burd's overbearing nature extended to his home life – one young female servant having allegedly thrown herself from the Stirling Bridge as a consequence of his harsh treatment. The rumour that she carried his child cannot be qualified, and may simply be the result of local gossips attempting to further demonise a reviled rogue.

In 1773, this disgraceful situation having been brought to public notice by protesting councillors and Incorporations, the Court of Session declared September's Stirling election void, it 'having been brought about by undue influence and corrupt practices'. The 'Black Bondsmen' appealed against this judgement to the House of Lords, but to no avail. The Court suspended and subsequently dismissed the whole Council, appointing Dr John Gillespie, glass merchant John Glass Snr, and David Gourlay Esq., to further investigate the quagmire of mischief and misappropriation represented by the town's accounts and to manage the Burgh's affairs. Foremost amongst their duties was the appointment of new Bailies. Burgesses were disqualified from participating in parliamentary elections, from doing business with the Convention of Royal Burghs, and from appointing Deacons of the Trades or a Dean of Guild. It's prestige tarnished, and its ability to trade with other towns effectively hobbled, the Burgh's privileges were not restored – after an appeal costing the town £100 – until 1781. Even then the election of new Councillors and Bailies was overseen by the Sheriff Deputes of Perthshire and Lanarkshire. The 'Bondsmen' were fined, but the Burgh they had sworn to serve paid the greater price of their villainy.

The Courts

Before properly considering the crimes and punishments of auld Stirling we should first attend to the courts in which various offences were tried.

The Burgh Court

As described in the previous section, this was composed of five magistrates – four Bailies appointed from the Council, and the Provost – any two of whom might be selected to sit upon the Bench at a given time. Rotation of posts ensured (in theory, at least) that at least one magistrate with previous experience was present. Other key personnel included the Town Clerk, whose principal responsibilities included recording proceedings and advising the Bailies (who generally had little or no legal training) on the business of the Court, and the Procurator Fiscal. As his title suggests, the Fiscal's original role was little more than the collection of fines. This service was superseded, as a consequence of the *Criminal Procedure Act* of 1701, by an increased role in the investigation and prosecution of offences on behalf of both the Burgh and Sheriff Courts. An agent for the defence would usually be present, but juries rarely participated. In one notable exception, in 1629, Bailies were so exasperated by the constant lies and obfuscations offered by James Ramsey's band of 'idle and sturdy vagabonds, common thieves, evil liars and haunters and resorters of evil company', lifted for stealing and re-selling plaids, that they decided a public example must be made of the miscreants – and engaged a full fifteen-man jury to sanction their subsequent scourging, branding and banishment. There was little need for a courtroom: this was a civil court dealing with minor cases of theft, or crimes against public order, and trials would ordinarily occur within any available small chamber. Jury trials only became commonplace in the wake of the 'Black Bond' embarrassment, when the Bailies were under greater pressure to show that their duties were being exercised fairly and with full observance of due process. More serious offences – fraud, murder, and so forth – would be referred to Edinburgh's Court of Sessions (Scotland's High Court) or the Circuit Court (see

Ever vigilant: this Medieval representation of Justice, now on display in the Bastion beneath the Thistles shopping centre, once stood over the entrance to the Tolbooth. (Photo by David Kinnaird, courtesy of the Thistles shopping centre)

page 36). While, in theory, the Burgh Court had the power of life or death over those brought before it, this right was rarely exercised. Fines, corporal punishment and banishment were the norm.

Weel ken't faces – known citizens of the Burgh – would generally be permitted to remain at liberty during proceedings. This might seem uncommonly trusting, but in an enclosed community it was simple common sense to assume that citizens on trial would not pre-empt the most extreme punishment for non-capital crimes – banishment – and run away. Most had nowhere else to go. Vagrants and outsiders, on the other hand, would be thrown into the Tolbooth until such time as the complaints against them were processed. This, as John G. Harrison notes, could pose problems for the poor. 'A possibility…was that a complaint might be made and they imprisoned, but the complainant would take no further action.' In such cases 'it was very difficult to get out again'. Occasionally the parsimony of the council could work to the advantage of the accused, as was the case, in 1677, for supposed witches Jannet Craig, Janet McNair, John Gray, and Mary and Thomas Michell. The charge, that they had used enchantments to drown the sons of a neighbour, were almost certainly malicious, but they were only judged to be so after Bailies complained to the Privy Council about the great cost to the town of detaining them in the Tolbooth without trial for fifteen weeks.

ET in Arcadia ego? A pretty pastoral scene painted onto the plaster of one eighteenth-century Tolbooth chamber. Until the 1780s, most trials would have occurred, without juries, in these small rooms. (Photo by David Kinnaird)

STIRLING
(From the Terrace)
Published by Dunt Miller, Bookseller

The Municipal Boundary – The Black Boy fountain and Port Street viewed from Pitt Terrace, *c.* 1860. The Barras Yett, gallows and Burgh Wall long since removed, this remained the often uneasy judicial boundary between the Burgh and Sheriff Courts. (Author's collection)

The Sheriff Court

This also sat in Stirling (though not always within the Tolbooth) but covered a largely rural jurisdiction, to which those prosecuted by 'franchise courts' – private courts of local lairds and landowners, established during the reign of David I, and not discontinued until the eighteenth century – had right of appeal. Territorial disputes, regarding which areas of the Burgh or what fines were under the control of the Council-controlled Burgh Court and which fell under the auspices of the Sheriff, were not uncommon – a situation not helped by the Procurator Fiscal, who had responsibility to both judiciaries, being appointed by the Sheriff. In one case from the 1720s a man convicted by the Sheriff was detained within the Tolbooth, pending punishment. The Bailies recognised their obligation of incarceration, but refused to feed him: he wasn't *their* prisoner. There followed a lengthy and increasingly recursive correspondence between the Bailie, the Sheriff and the prisoner's counsel regarding who was responsible for what, why and when. As the Courts chased their tails, the convict – whose subsequent execution probably came as a merciful release – was slowly wasting away. Unlike the Burgh Court the participation of juries was commonplace. The Sheriff Court continues to the present day as the ordinary civil court in Scotland.

The Circuit Justiciary Court

From the middle years of the seventeenth century the Circuit Court would sit in the Tolbooth. Under the control of the High Court of Justiciary, and – presided over by a properly appointed scarlet and ermine-clad Judge – this dealt with the most serious of crimes, and might consider cases from the Burgh, the Sheriffdom or, indeed, any part of central Scotand. Initially sittings were only once a year, though this had become a quarterly visitation by the end of the eighteenth century. While the Burgh and Sheriff Courts had power to enforce corporal punishments and banishments, the Justiciary could (and commonly did) extend punishment to transportation (initially to the Americas, then, following commencement of the American Revolutionary War, in 1776, Australia), or death. While cases dealt with by this Court are rare within these pages, those that do feature fully demonstrate its power.

The Commissary Court

Of little interest in so far as criminal prosecutions are concerned, Commissary Courts were established in Scotland between 1564 and 1566 as a replacement for former consistorial courts whereby Bishops exercised civil jurisdiction in issues relating to marriage, divorce, bastardy and inheritance. Lesser Commissary Courts were soon established, their powers including occasional actions for personal injury, recovery of debts up to £40 and slander. In consideration of this latter offence one Stirling tradition, noted by J.S. Fleming in *Old Nooks of Stirling* (1898), involved the slanderer being marched through the street of the town to the door of their accuser, 'upon Sonday nextocum befoir the processioun, sark alane, and ane walx canddill in her hand' [*sic*]. Public exposure, before the congregation, 'sark alane' (wearing only a shirt), provided humiliation and a symbolic vulnerability to the light of truth represented by the 'walx canddill'. Brought before the citizen they had wronged, they would be confronted with the declaration, 'False tongue, thou lied' and a summary of their slander, before being made to kneel before their former victim, 'heid boweit and baret', at the Tron or Mercat Cross, and to beg their forgiveness.

At least until the mid-seventeenth century the Commissary often relied less on hard evidence in establishing guilt or innocence than on the number of character witnesses able to testify as to the truthfulness and good character of the contending parties – witnesses, often, who had not witnessed the deeds or crimes considered there. This was a throwback to the Medieval system of conflict resolution, *Trial by Compurgation*, which operated on the crude principle that witnesses swore to the truth of their account upon the Bible, and that no one would willingly risk their immortal soul by swearing falsely before God: if more swore to the good character of one party than another, then subjective 'truth' would be established. When conducted in the presence of a Bishop, and dramatically iterated by the pomp and power of the Roman Catholic Church, this threat of damnation for perjury may have carried considerably more weight than it did in post-Reformation Scotland, where the local Minister warned each week of the fundamental concupiscence of the citizenry. Guilt was not necessarily presumed, in this new age of faith, but participants were under greater pressure to provide *proof* and give substance to their suits. The kirk and courts could agree that 'In God we trust' – but everyone else needed an alibi.

Another early punishment exercised by the early Commissary Court and inherited exclusively by the Kirk Session, was the withdrawal of burial rights. Tradition tells of the quarrelsome eighteenth-century Blackburn brothers, both entitled to bury their kin within the family's heritable lair within the Holy Rude. As one half of the family interred their ilk, the other would invariably appear to disrupt proceedings – presumably with the intention of scaring off their rivals

Sober as a Judge: the former Judge's robing room has found new life as the Tolbooth's theatre bar. (Photo by David Kinnaird)

Trial by compurgation: a recreation of a civil trial in the grounds of Stirling Castle in 1990. (Photo courtesy of the Heritage Events Company)

and gaining sole rights to the plot. On one occasion, after several attempts to reconcile the brothers, the Minister was himself assaulted. His response was to immediately withdraw burial rights from both factions. In an era of high mortality, families unable to plant their kin within the Burgh had no choice but to move on. The Blackburns became someone else's problem.

By the 1830s, the major powers of the Commissary Courts were absorbed by the Court of Session, the functions of the Lesser Commissaries having already been transferred to local Sheriffs a decade earlier.

The Staffman

In the performance of public punishment the principal functionary of Stirling's various courts was, for several centuries, The Staffman: official torturer and executioner to the Burgh. The title itself appears to be attributable solely to the ceremonial staff presented to this officer of the court on his appointment, the earliest reference to which is an entry in the Burgh Treasurer's books from June 1652, which records the sum of eight shillings paid to incumbent executioner William Lapsley for provision of 'ane staff'. The term occurs nowhere else in Scottish tradition, its distinctiveness to the area confirmed by the only available dictionary definition of the term, from the *Concise Scottish Dictionary* (1985) – 'Staffman – the BURGH hangman, seventeenth century. Stirling' – though the title and duties appear to have been well established some decades before Lapsley's appointment. As we shall shortly see, certain terms and conditions of employment hint at a much greater antiquity.

On the surface the executioner's lot, if not a happy one, was certainly extremely comfortable by the standards of the day. The same Treasurer's records note that Maister Lapsley was due a yearly salary, or *fial*, of 10s weekly, and a further 13s 4d for each cowing, carting, nailing, scourging or similar sundry act of court-sanctioned strife. An impressive £1 15s 4d was paid for each execution, rising rapidly to £4 within a few decades (including the cost of a post-mortem meal for the hungry hangman). This increase is, as J.S. Fleming reassuringly notes in *Old Nooks of Stirling*, a likely 'consequence of these becoming fewer by reason of more enlightened civilization'. He was provided, too, at public expense, with an official residence – a first floor dwelling above the municipal stables in the appropriately named Hangman's Close – as well as coal and candles. He was entitled to a handful of corn (otherwise known as a *goupin* or *lock* – from which the term *Lockman* was often assigned to Scots hangmen until the nineteenth century) from each farmer at the weekly Meal and Butter Market, and allowed a similar toll of ale or wine from local tavern-keepers – with the stern stipulation, according to Victorian historian and raconteur William Drysdale, in his *Old Faces, Old Places and Old Stories of Stirling*, that he 'durst not...sit down in their company, but that he had to quaff the contents of his Quaich standing, and then retire'. With more than twenty taverns within the Burgh Wall, it was decided that this was a privilege restricted to only *one* public house each day, thus allowing the town's landlords to share the burden of the bully's thirst, and prevent any particular tavern from suffering the stigma of being on too-familiar terms with so loathed a local figure. The instrument by which such tributes were collected, the *Staffman's Caup* (cup), or *Haddis Cog*, is the only part of the executioner's regalia to survive, and is on public display to this day within Stirling's Smith Art Gallery and Museum. He was provided, too, with an official livery consisting, originally, of a half-grey cloth doublet and breeches, shirts, shoes, and a blue bonnet. The tally for 'cloathes and furnisching to Marteine the executioner' (Lapsley's short-lived predecessor), in April 1651, was a staggering £19 1s 4d. This livery appears to have endured until at least 1708, when the last 'blew bonnet' was ordered (for 10s 6d), but by the middle of the eighteenth century a rather more fetching wardrobe was in evidence, consisting of yellow stockings, black plush or velvet breeches, a yellow waistcoat and a dark green frock-coat, its

The Staffman's Cup: the last
surviving artefact of the Burgh
executioner, the 'Hangman's Caup'
allowed him free corn or grain at the
weekly markets. (Photo reproduced
by kind permission of the Stirling
Smith Art Gallery & Museum)

seams lined with narrow yellow worsted piping, topped by a black cocked hat, and
accessorized – as all fashionably fearsome functionaries should surely be – with a
large silver-handled clasp-knife, attached by a hempen coil to a girdle around his
waist. The purpose of the knife will shortly become apparent.

The tools of the Staffman's trade – the Cuck Stool (stocks), Jougs and one-ankle
Fetter Bolt, Thumikins (thumbscrews), irons and coals (for brandings) – as well as
'towes, small cordes and tweine' and the cost of any other incidental expenses or
assistance incurred during public punishments – were also paid for by the Burgh,
as were fees quite unrelated to his civic duties: records from July 1709 note the 12s
paid to John Steill 'for sueping the Staffman's lum' (chimney), and an entry from
Michelmas 1724 records the sum of £2 paid 'for a coffine to the Staffman's bastard,
and a winning sheet thereto.'

There was, of course, a catch – several, if truth be told. The residence at
Hangman's Close – a dismal building predating (in the opinion of Fleming) the
jail-house to which it was attached by many centuries, and now long demolished
– was described by William Drysdale (writing, admittedly, in the late nineteenth
century, by which time the property was a virtual ruin, serving as a Night Shelter
for vagrants) as 'a mere apology for a human habitation, many a stable in the town

Hangman's Close. The town executioner
enjoyed free lodging at the Burgh's expense.
(Illustration by David Kinnaird, based on an
original sketch by R. S. Fleming)

being said to be more comfortable'. A rather more onerous condition of service is
revealed in another entry from the Burgh records – this time from 1633 – regarding
the appointment of an earlier Staffman, Thomas Grant:

> 20 May, 1633. – Thomas Grant, Born in Geenalmond, under David Murray of
> Bulhindye, ressavit and sworne servand and executioner to this town of Stirling his
> life tyme, and sall not remove or absent himself aff the toune, but by licence of the
> Magistrate, under pane of daithe.

This fatally restrictive *'life tyme'* appointment was a not uncommon device by which
the services of an unpopular but functionary – a *'necessary man'*, as the Staffman
is grudgingly termed in one eighteenth-century record – could be guaranteed
in medieval municipalities. This may hint at the ancient origins of the Staffman's
role. Executioners were occasionally appointed from the ranks of the condemned:
their lives extended only so long as they might continue to serve the courts. This
selection process may seem morally questionable to modern eyes. With typical
Victorian indignance R. S. Fleming was outraged by the notion, railing that it elicits
'wonder that any person, however criminal or degraded, could be found willing to

accept this repulsive office on such fearful terms'. Actually, it is purely pragmatic, both on the part of the would-be executioner – for whom the practical benefits of accepting the perquisites and restrictions of service (chief amongst which was that they remained alive) far outweighed the unpleasant alternative – and for the authorities, mercifully freed from getting their genteel hands dirty. And, while dirt is on our minds, it is worth noting that when there were no executions, whippings or sundry punishments to occupy the Staffman, he was to be gainfully employed in sweeping the streets and clearing gutters.

The aforementioned Thomas Grant was no such desperate villain, having already proven his talents as executioner to the feared Laird of Glenalmond, who – until the *Heritable Jurisdictions Act* (1746), enforced after the 1745 Jacobite Rebellion, removed the feudal authorities of clan chieftains – enjoyed the power of 'furca and fossa' (or 'pit and gallow') over his tenants. Many Stirling Staffman were similarly qualified, and the post was rarely empty. Local tradition has it that in the absence of an appointed executioner or torturer, the Bailies might themselves be called upon to steep themselves in the sanguinary mechanism of ultimate judicial sanction, and perform executions themselves. It is likely that this consideration troubled those sitting on the Bench in 1652, during one such vacancy, whose efforts to solicit the temporary services of the Culross hangman were frustrated by the childish behaviour of two of their Council rivals, William Spittal and Walter Cowane (himself a former Bailie, and brother of Stirling's celebrated benefactor). An entry in the Burgh Records from 4 October tells the tale:

> A complaint is made by James Sword and William Smythe against Walter Cowane and William Spittall, schawing that they be employit by the Magistrates to go to Culros for the executioner to attend heir the tyme of the sitting of the Justice Court, the said Walter and William did mock and scorne them; quilk they acknowledgit and cam in will for the same.

The pair were to soon to pay the price, literally and metaphorically, for flouting the authority of the Court: they were sharply bidden:

> To convoy and put hombe the said executioner to Culros upon their awin charges [their own expense], and to return the tounes band and the morne at night under the pane of ane hundred pundis money.

There must have been some amusement to be had from the bill presented to them by the Bailies, which included £1 4s to 'a man that was directed to Culros to try whether the hangman there wes alive or not', £4 19s 8d 'for a pair of breechis to the executioner' (who was, it seems, in good health after all), expenses of £14 2s for

Messrs Sword and Smythe (who, by all accounts, 'travellit weill' as they oversaw the engagement of the executioner and accompanied him to Stirling), and £6 2s to the unnamed hangman, which included 'drink money at the execution'.

The Stirling Staffman, similarly, might be loaned out to other parishes in need. In 1781 (by which time the Staffman James Cuthill's annual *fial* had risen to £9 2s 6d), the Bailies considered a request for his services from the managers of the Carron Company (the region's most important ironworks):

> Praying that the Staffman may be allowed to go to Carron works to execute a sentence of the Justices of the Peace upon a person who stole goods from the Company. They grant the desire thereof, provided Mr Campbell the company's agent grant a bond upon stamped paper to the Town Treasurer binding himself to pay the Town five hundred merks Scots money unless the Staffman is returned safe and sound.

As we will see later, with the sad tale of Baird and Hardie, the punishment of anyone who sinned against the mighty Carron Company was a political as much as a criminal matter, and Stirling's Bailies were eager to protect their asset in the face of possible public strife.

'The Last Limb o' the Law'

Cuthill was, it seems, the last to bear the official title of Staffman, a claim to fame often inaccurately attributed to his predecessor in the post, John (more popularly, Jock) Rankine – an error to which this author must confess to repeating, in his own *Haunted Stirling*. Though the son of an Ayrshire executioner, and well experienced in his chosen trade, Jock appears to have achieved infamy as a consequence of his quite staggering ineptitude. According to William Drysdale, he was the favoured victim of youthful rowdies, or *kail-runts*, who were:

> More frequently found, and…in greater number, in the neighbourhood of Jock's door than of any other of the inhabitants, the spirit of mischief leading [them] to devote more of their time and attention to him, in the hope of greater sport being obtained by reason of his eccentricity.

In the winter of 1760, Jock called upon a peculiar and rarely invoked privilege due to the Staffman, and requested that the Burgh find him a wife. The object of his amour was an Irishwoman, a petty thief and occasional prostitute named Isabella Kilconquhar (known variously as 'Tibbie Cawker' or 'Canker' to her neighbours, who – according to tradition – found her Irish brogue near-impenetrable), then serving a term within the Tolbooth jail for the theft of laundry from a clothes line near the Linlithgow Bridge (then within Stirling's legal jurisdiction). The prospect of the union between two such gormless grotesques greatly amused the local populace. They were joined together on the very day of her release from prison, the town turned out in merry mood as the happy hangman and his bride-to-be were accompanied by four halberd-bearing Town Officers in full regalia, to be joined together by Provost Jaffray – in his capacity as Justice of the Peace.

The *kail-runts* had planned their own unique celebration of the Staffman's nuptials. As the newlyweds snuggled down together in Hangman's Close, the brats heaped as much dung as they could carry from the stables below around their doorway, leaving it to harden in the cold night air – requiring Jock and Tibbie to exit via their first-floor window, the next morning.

Although we must, by all accounts, pity the poor brow-beaten beldame – as frequent a subject of her husband's ire as any local rogue assigned to his questionable care by the courts – Tibbie herself was a regular source of embarrassment both to Jock and to the town. A report by William McAllister, Commander of the Town Guard, dated 3 November 1762, records:

> A theft committed last night by some persons in the house of Widow Young, and the guard being applied to search the Hangman's House, found one Jean Taylor from Torbrex, and the Hangman's wife, and on search found the shirts that had been stolen and nine bottles of ale and some cheese…

Tibbie, of course, denied any part in this felonious filching. The Bailies believed not a word, and bid that:

> Jean Taylor be whipped through the town by the hands of the Hangman receiving the usual number of stripes at the accustomed places on her naked back, betwixt the hour of eleven and twelve forenoon, and continues advising us to the other woman till then, and appoints both of them to be carried back to the Workhouse.

It was too much to ask, one imagines, that even a garrulous gowk like Jock be required to endure the laughter of his neighbours as he publicly whipped *his own wife* through the streets of the town.

Rankine was known to supplement his income by acting as a debt collector on behalf of various local dignitaries, including the pompous Reverend Turner, Minister of the parish between 1740 and 1762, who bid Jock act as his Factor in recovery of arrears due to him from a stipend on the Ochils property of the Laird of Loss. One might imagine that the town torturer turning up at one's door would fill even one possessed of the bravest of hearts with dread. Loss paid on the spot, but

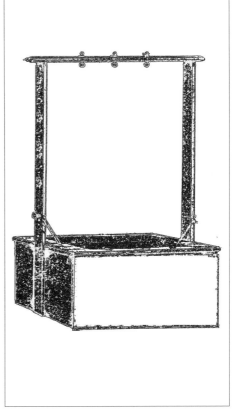

Above left The Hangman's wayward wife: Isabella 'Tibbie Cawker' (actress Patricia Brannigan) was the cause of considerable embarrassment for her Staffman spouse. (Photo by David Kinnaird)

Above right The gallows tree: The traditional Scots Gib was little more than a tilting-frame. The condemned would climb a ladder then be 'throw off' – slowly strangling before the mob. (Illustration by David Kinnaird)

not through fear. By all accounts the Laird was so amused by the lack of subtlety demonstrated by the dour divine's employment of the shabby, stammering Staffman as his debt-collector, that he insisted on writing out a receipt for the illiterate Jock to affix his mark – and amused his friends by presenting this tatty scrawl as proof of his brush with the *'Last Limb o' the Law'* for years thereafter. Maister Rankine was never again engaged on such errands.

Much of Jock Rankine's enduring legacy – the inspiration for his continuing characterisations within the Stirling Old Town Jail visitor attraction (based within the restored 1847 County Jail since 1996), and on the *Stirling GhostWalk* guided tours of the Burgh – relies upon the popularity of two colourful accounts of his exploits contained within the pages of Drysdale's popular histories of the town.

The first relates to the disgraceful proceedings of the execution of Sarah Cameron, a young woman condemned to hang for throwing her illegitimate newborn from the Stirling Bridge into the torrent of the Rover Forth. The gib erected by the Barras Yett was, as already noted in Chapter One, of the traditional Scots style of the era. After looping, hooking and tying the noose, Rankin is said to have struggled to push his victim's ladder away from the frame. According to William Drysdale, the terrified lass somehow seized hold of the beam, preventing the ladder from shifting, and, despite the efforts of the aged and incompetent hangman, could not be persuaded to release her trembling, white-knuckled grip. Unfortunately for Sarah, grim aid was on hand:

> Attending the sad scene were the town officers with their halberts, and one of them, Tom Bone, seeing the dilemma, went deliberately up, and gave the woman's fingers several knocks with his halbert, which caused her to let go, and Rankin succeeded in pushing her off. A good deal of sympathy was expressed for the woman, but Bone's vulgar and inhuman interference incurred the dire displeasure of the juvenile and female portion of the community, and he had to be escorted to a place of safety until the affair blew over.

Jock's pitiful performance has endured in popular memory – unfortunately so, given that the story is almost complete bunkum. For all his faults, the calamities accompanying Mistress Cameron's ignominious exit from this world simply *cannot* be attributed to him. The poor girl was executed for child-murder, that much is not in doubt. There is some anecdotal indication that her illegitimate offspring was stillborn, so the appropriateness of the charge laid against her will certainly seem questionable to modern readers. If unmarried, or if in service – where pregnancy would invariably have seen the unfortunate serving-girl cast out on the street – the young woman would most likely have made every effort to conceal her condition, and to give birth alone. Abandonment of illegitimate offspring was commonplace, and neo-natal mortality high. Were her secret shame to be discovered, 'the childe being found dead or amissing', prosecution for child-murder was inevitable. Mercifully, many just like her were spared the gallows: juries often delivering (uniquely Scottish) *Not Proven* verdicts. Witnessed disposing of the evidence of her delivery, by throwing her child into the river, Sarah Cameron was bound to hang, but the date of her despatch is recorded as 29 October 1784 – by which time Jock had not been in office for some thirteen and a half years. Cameron, whose tale engendered much public pity, was most likely despatched by James Cuthill, and it seems highly unlikely that an executioner whose brutal effectiveness enjoyed sufficient renown to bring him to the attention of the Magistrates and Managers of Ayr and the Carron Company, would have botched so *simple* a job. Drysdale was a committed antiquarian and passionate populariser of the minutiae of local history, and *Old Faces, Old Places and Old Stories of Stirling* is a treasure-trove of riotous reminiscences of Burgh life which might otherwise be lost to us, but his passion for the quaint and the couthy often led him to rely far too heavily on unreliable (if entertaining) anecdote. His greatest contribution to Rankine's enduring mythology is his amusing account of Jock and Tibbie's 'cat and mouse' marriage, the last incident of which is described thus:

> One day, and that a Sabbath, a disturbance took place, and Jock, though an old man, determined to give his wife a thrashing. Tibbie had the good fortune to elude him and took refuge in a neighbour's house. Returning to his dwelling, he seized a basin of cold soup, which he greedily drank, but it so happened that a small bone stuck in his throat and ultimately choked him…

A hangman choking to death? A dish laden with a *soupson* too much of dramatic irony. According to William, Tibbie returned to the Close just in time to witness her husband's passing: 'with exemplary affection and tenderness [she] tended him in his last moments, and did her utmost to alleviate his sufferings'.

Touching – but, again, total *tosh*. A popular adjunct to this tale has it that Tibbie deliberately *placed* the fatal chicken bone in her husband's broth. Neither story has a single word of truth. Stirling Town Council Minutes for 2 February 1771 relate a very different, and somehow less satisfying, end to the Staffman's career:

> The Council Considering, that John Rankine the present Staffman, Is not only upon occasions when necessity Calls unable to execute his Office, but also that he and his Wife keep a Bad House in the Night-time by entertaining Tinkers and Vagabonds and having quarrels with them to the great annoyance and nuisance of the Neighbourhood. They therefore dismiss him as Staffman, and appoint the Sheriff to give him Ten Shillings Sterling, money for paying the expense of Carrying him and his Wife to Glasgow or elsewhere.

Many a Town Officer (many a Bailie, too, as we have already seen) was guilty of far more serious misdemeanours than the 'annoyance and nuisance' of their neighbours. Was there, perhaps, some more serious or shameful reason for Jock's sudden dismissal. Could Tibbie have been up to her old larcenous tricks once again – or was the hangman himself complicit in her crimes? The Bailies would certainly be reluctant to have the agent of their justified judicial ire exposed as a criminal. We shall never know. The popular account of the hangman choking to death has become entrenched in local lore – reported as *fact* as recently as 2010, in Marie Brammeld's edition of *The Vagabond Book of Stirling*.

Hanged for child-murder: The death of Sarah Cameron (actress Patricia Brannigan) was not-so-swift as that promised by the drop-gallows, pictured in this scene from a recreation of her execution featured in the 1999 Stirling GhostWalk. (Photo by Allan Goldie)

Night Shelter: the Staffman's House, St John Street, around 1900. Parents urged local children to avoid danger in the adjoining doss-house by spinning tall tales of Jock Rankin's spectre. (Author's collection)

Drysdale's accounts, and the mysterious mechanisms of storytelling, have entrenched the colourful comic grotesque of the (second-last) *Staffman* into other evolving legends. Generations of local bairns were warned to avoid the gloomy high-walled huddle of Hangman's Close, lest they be set upon by Rankin's wraith – his spectre's oft-reported gagging growl explained away as an eternal effort to dislodge the fatal fowl-bone from his ghoulish gullet – a tale almost certainly devised by anxious parents eager to discourage their offspring from playing near the vagrants' Night Shelter, which occupied the derelict Close well into the early years of the twentieth century.

Between the execution of Sarah Cameron, in 1784, and the last public hanging – that of farmer Allan Mair (whose tale we shall return to in due course) – in October 1843, there were a mere fifteen executions in Stirling. Within those few short decades transportation and a more formalised practice of sentencing and servitude – along with the *'more enlightened civilization'* so prized by the worthy Mr Fleming – displaced the public punishments which had provided the Staffman with his trade. Between the last execution on the *Gallous Mauling*, in 1788, and the installation of new gib nearby the Tolbooth in Broad Street, in 1811 – a gap of nearly thirteen years – the office of Staffman appears to have been dissolved, James Cuthill being the last to be referred to as such in public records. The executioner and town-torturer as a regular part of local life was, mercifully for the population, a thing of the past, his duties now performed by a more select, professional fraternity whose rare services could be solicited – at a price – by communities such as that of the Royal Burgh only under the direst of circumstances.

The Town Officers

A more enduring, if somewhat less notorious, manifestation of the mechanism of public order, one which lasted – albeit largely in symbolic and ceremonial terms – into the twentieth century, is represented by the Town Officers. There were six in total: a drummer, a piper and four *halberdiers*. These operated under the authority of a Marshall, usually a Bailie or his designated agent, and provided the Provost and Councillors with a defensive honour-guard, marching before them at ceremonial or public events. A piper and drummer had long been on the public payroll, the former to provide entertainment at markets and festivals, the latter to 'keep tyme' and help advertise proclamations and new regulations 'by tuck of drum, that none may pretend ignorance thereof' (a similar function was served by the Bellman, or Town Crier, at the Mercat Cross). In 1642, Duncan Ewing was paid an impressive yearly *fial* of £60 Scots 'to tuck his drum nightly at seven hours and every morning at four hours, beginning at Lady Vennell and from there through the whole town', and provided with a distinctive red livery soon to be shared by the other Officers.

Jock Rankin Lives! The 'Last Limb o' the Law' still entertains visitors to the Stirling Old Town Jail. (Photo courtesy of Stirling District Tourism)

Town Officers: the distinctive red cashmere livery of these early law officers can be seen each day in the Bastion, beneath the Thistles shopping centre. (Photo by David Kinnaird, courtesy of the Thistles shopping centre)

An established part of public life by the early seventeenth century, they certainly dressed to impress. In 1622 the Burgh Treasurer was authorised to purchase for each officer, 'a garment of red English cashmere, viz coat, breeks and shanks, with white trimmings, wrought in good fashion'. The only surviving example of this dashingly distinctive apparel (though dating only from the early twentieth century) is on public display daily within the sixteenth-century Bastion beneath the Thistles mall. By the eighteenth century a distinctive cocked hat had been added to their regalia along with a sword and halberd or *Lochaber Axe*. Stirling was an important sword-making town in the eighteenth century, so it was only logical that the Officers should display the Burgh's wares: in 1738 each was presented with a new brass-handled blade at a cost of £6, each, to the public purse. The protective basket hilts for these fine weapons were the work of Walter Allan, newly-appointed Deacon of the Hammermen. In the wake of the 1745-46 Jacobite Rebellion, the *Act of Proscription* of 1746 – described by English wit Dr Samuel Johnson as 'the last act by which the Highlanders are deprived of their arms' – Scottish citizens were prohibited from bearing weapons, wearing traditional highland garb (the kilt and clan colours), and from the teaching of Gaelic and the playing of '*martial*

Honour Guard: the Town Officers' ceremonial functions were retained long after their constabulary role in local affairs were forgotten, as in this Provostorial pronouncement in 1901. (Photo courtesy of James Munn)

pipes' (bagpipes). Most of these prohibitions had little effect on largely Lowland sensibilities of staunchly Protestant Stirling, which had little sympathy for the causes and culture of the Highland Catholic clansmen and their figurehead Prince Charles Edward Stuart, and bore bitter memories of the brutal rule of 'truck and drum' by which the Young Pretender's men held the Burgh during their brief occupation of the town, in January 1746. One local consequence of Proscription (aside from the sudden slump in trade suffered by Deacon Allan and his ilk, who were embarrassed by public knowledge that they had enjoyed considerable custom with the rebel clans immediately prior to 'The 45'), was that Stirling's Town Officers ranked amongst the few non-military personnel in Scotland still permitted to bear arms.

Their swords were, however, largely for show. The halberd, on the other hand – most easily described as a steel spike and axe-blade mounted on a long shaft – was essential to their public role. A decorous but formidable weapon, it was a much-prized instrument of civil defence. During the previous century each Trade or Guild member had been ordered to make personal provision of such a weapon, or risk a fine of £5 Scots. In 1663 the Treasurer was appointed to 'send to Holland for twenty new halberds for the townis use.'

It was a distinction to be selected from the ranks of the Town Guard (later known as the Burgh Militia) – of which it was the duty of every able-bodied adult male to serve at one time or another – and elevated, usually through the patronage of a burgess or Bailie, for paid service as a Town Officer. Records for 1683 note various sums, for example, 'Payit to Patrik Myller, at Robert Burne, Baillie, his direction ', including 6s 8d for 'straw for his bed', 3s 4d for 'mending the key to his dore' and a 'fial' – 'payed him weiklie 13s, 4d, the space of 22 weikis'. If these prerquisites bring to mind the indulgences offered to the Staffman, we should not be surprised, as the role of the Town Officers was more than to provide pomp and circumstance at civic functions – the same tally of monies due to good Master Myller included 12s 'payit to him for scurgeing a theif' (we shall discuss *Scourging* and other popular punishments shortly). Often the Officers worked in tandem with the Staffman, as in this case from February 1698:

> Item, to the officers for standing at the cross tuo hours till Margaret Graham, ane adultress, was cowed in the head and convoying hir out of toun with the Staffman
> £2 8s 0d
> Item, to the staffman for coweing her and conveying hir out of towne
> £1 1s 0d

The Officers' role was to ensure that public order was maintained while the Staffman did his unpleasant and unpopular duty: a necessary function given the high passions certain punishments prompted in the local population – as would often have been

Men at arms: the Halberds, or 'Lochaber Axes', carried by the Town Officers. These formidable blades would be fixed on a 6ft shaft. (Photo by David Kinnaird, courtesy of the Thistles shopping centre)

the case with instances of ritual humiliation such as that detailed above, where a defenceless woman would be 'cowed' (her head roughly shaven in a public place). The Staffman's safety was, of course, not their sole consideration. Often they acted as escorts, accompanying troublemakers out of town, or ensuring that prisoners themselves were free from unnecessary abuse from the mocking or malicious mob while under restraint. The Drummer or Piper called the townsfolk's attention, and provided necessary pacing for punishment, while the *halberdiers* kept them under control. A few random selections from Burgh records details their duties in fairly representative fashion. June 1652 saw them 'putting away out of the toune ane old vagabond wife that had a dumb bairne, and syndrie other beggaris'. In April 1654 they were 'payit at the bayleyis orders for carting a woman taken through the town 'branket'' (wearing a 'Branks' or 'Scold's Bridle' – a traditional humiliation offered to troublesome wives). The sum of £3 6s, paid on 14 October 1699 to four Officers for 'convoying Robertt and John Alders and John Spaden to the gallous, quhor two of their lugs were cut out and they burnt on the brow', would tend to indicate either the cost incurred by increased risk to the Officers' own safety, or that they themselves – as was occasionally the case (as we saw with Master Myller) – had to inflict the prescribed punishment.

The Town Officers were often at the heart of civic strife, but not always on the side of law and order. In 1706, following a moonlight raid on the home of the Laird of Innermay, near Perth, a gang of housebreakers led by John Murray, fled to Stirling, and to the lodging of soldier, Neil Glass. Here they were taken by the Town Officers, who bundled them into the Tolbooth – and promptly helped themselves to a share of the gang's burglarious spoils, which included silverware, the Laird's watch and 35 guineas in cash. The unexpected restless liquidity of the Officers, witnessed shortly afterwards in the local taverns, soon alerted the authorities to their mischief. They were dismissed on the spot. One of Murray's minions, a thug named McWattie, quickly escaped – only to be re-captured by one of the disgraced Officers, who was promptly given his job back as a reward. Careless 'light fingeredness' is a frequently noted fault of Officers of this era: another of their ilk having been ritually stripped of his livery at the Mercat Cross, that same year, for conspiring to steal masonry from the steeple of the Holy Rude kirk to be re-sold as gravestones.

In another case, from 17 December 1767, one Mary Canker, a native of Linlithgow, was:

> Committed prisoner to the Tollbooth of Stirling, upon a warrant from the Provost for behaving in an indecent manner with James Drummond, the Town Drummer, and otherways behaving ill during the night foresaid.

An entertaining evening was clearly had by the percussive pup, as the same entry records that local weaver's daughter, Margaret Douglas, was 'convened for the same fault as Mary Canker the night foresaid'. Whatever punishment the Drummer received (if *any* – responsibility for such riotous revels was invariably placed firmly at the feet of the fairer sex) is not recorded. Mary and Margaret were spared the added insult to injury of being drummed out of town by their beau by choosing to 'voluntarily banish' themselves from the Royal Burgh. Marie Brammeld raises the intriguing possibility that the aforementioned Mary Canker *might* be the *sister* of Jock Rankin's spouse, Isabella – children named Isabel and Mary were certainly born to George Canker and Janet Dalrymple in Linlithgow, in 1729 and 1735 respectively, and it was for stealing clothes from a washing-line nearby the Linlithgow Bridge that 'Tibbie' was incarcerated in the Tolbooth. Jock's bride – referred to variously as 'Cawker' or 'Kilconquhar' – is generally believed to have been of Irish origin, which makes such a family connection unlikely, but, as the lesson of William Drysdale's merry musings makes clear, received wisdom is not always to be relied upon.

As with the Staffman, the decline of public punishments put an end to the Town Officer's role as instruments of public order or nascent law enforcement, assuming a purely ceremonial function in civic life – but outlasting that of the Staffman by more than a century.

3

BEGGARS, TRAMPS AND THIEVES

From the earliest times the preferred punishment if the Stirling Courts, and the one likely to best please the Burgh Treasurer, was the fine. For those unwilling, or more likely unable to pay the literal price of their sins, corporal punishment was the norm. A Council decree of 1702 decrees that 'such as can not or will not pay the pecuniary mulcts are to be punished in their persons'. R.S. Fleming's *Old Nooks of Stirling* helpfully draws our attention to an entry contained within the *Fragmenta Collecta*, a hodge-podge of ancient edicts and accounts of life in the Burgh prior to 1600. A strictly graduated system of penalties and punishments for theft was clearly in evidence in old Stirling, so strict in fact that Fleming was forced to observe that 'little was left to the discretion of the judge but to find the culprit guilty or innocent' – and, of course, to ascertain the value of the purloined property:

Giff ony be tane with the laff of a halfpenny in Brugh he aw throu the toune to be dungyn and fra a halfpenny vorth to iiij penijs he aw to be mair sairly dungyn. And for a pair of shone iiij penijs he aw to be put in the cuk stull an eftir that led to the hede of the toune and there shall forsuer the toune.

And fra iiij penijs to viij penihs and a farthing he sall be put upon the cuk stull, and eftir that sall be led to the hede of the toune, and that he at takk hym to cut his eyr of. And fra viij penijsand a farthing to xvi penijs and an oblous [shilling] he sall be set upon the cuk stull and eftir that led to the hede of the toune and thar he at tuk hym ha to cut his other eyr of.

And eftir that giff he be tane with viij penijs and a ferding he that tuks hym sall hing hym. Item for xxxij penijs and i oblous he that takis a man may hing hym. [*sic*]

Although prosecutions for theft are rarely recorded in records for the seventeenth and early eighteenth centuries, this passage is interesting for our purposes in that it indicates the principal means employed in punishing those who transgressed against or undermined the commonwealth of the community. These were, in turn, according to the increasing seriousness of the offence:

- Scourging
- The Cuck Stool (and Jougs)
- Banishment
- 'Lugging' (having one or both ears cut off) and
- Hanging

Other punishments were employed, but we shall attend to them in due course. The most important aspect of all such penalties is that justice should be *seen* to be done. It is easy for modern readers to be outraged by the severity of punishments frequently meted out by (or upon) our ancestors for the most seemingly trivial misdemeanours. Is it right or just that the theft of something valued at a few pennies (even taking account of inflation) should result in the culprit suffering the permanent disfigurement of having his ears cut off, or have his nose pinched with red hot irons? Of course not. In our outrage, however, we have the comfort of looking at the past from the perspective of a liberal, ordered, judicially consistent society. The past is very much a foreign country and, if we are to make any sense of its strange ways, we must quickly acknowledge not only that *they do things differently there*, but try to see *why*. Often the brutality of past punishments is – as Nicholas Humphrey aptly puts it in his 1987 introduction to E.P. Evans gloriously strange (and strangely insightful) *The Criminal Prosecution and Capital Punishment of Animals* (1906) – a desperate attempt to 'domesticate chaos' in the face of a disordered feudal world where laws, penalties, tolls and tributes might vary wildly from town to town, and where the likes of Staffman Thomas Grant's former employer, the Laird of Glenalmond, mentioned earlier, had the right *in liberam regalitatem* to dictate not only the nature of a given punishment, but to define what was or was not a crime.

The *public exhibition* of censure and penalty was seen as vital, both in terms of conspicuous societal revenge and as a deterrent to prospective future felons. To have an impact, to deter and to create order from chaos, the courts must publicly trumpet the *consequence* of crime – hence, as elsewhere in the kingdom, such punishments being enacted for maximum effect at points of access and egress to the town, such as the Barras Yett, or at the weekly Market Day. In Stirling this meant that chastisements increasingly occurred at the Tolbooth or Mercat Cross, where the Tron – the public scales or weighing mechanism (from the old French *trone*) – was located. Where better to balance the figurative scales of Justice than in a place of literal order and regulation?

Scourging

The most basic of penalties for theft was to be 'dungyn', or 'mair sairly dungyn' – that is scourged, or whipped through the town. Often this would employ the ritual of having one's arms bound to the rear of a cart which would be led, at a measured pace dictated by the beating of the Town Drum, from the Mercat Cross to the Barras Yett. Back stripped bare, criminals would be whipped throughout the short but painful journey, the cart often stopping at key points – such as churches, official residences, or the homes or businesses of those sinned against – in order to further reinforce the causal link between each individual crime and its summary punishment. The town itself, almost apart from its citizens, was a witness to the deed. In lesser cases the taws (or tawes), a shorter leather strap split into two tongues and toasted over a fire in order to harden the hide, might be employed by the Staffman. Variations of these foul objects remained in use within many Scottish schools as tools of corporal punishment well into the 1980s (though by that time, thankfully, only a minority of distinctly *old school* tutors were convinced of their appropriateness as a means

Scourge of Stirling: the staffman would often be called upon to whip thieves, beggars and vagabonds out of town. (Photo courtesy of Stirling District Tourism)

of maintaining classroom discipline – the tawes was banned completely in 1986). Records for 1683 note one such scourging, detailing the cost of the endeavour:

> Item, to the staffman for whipeing one man and tuo women throw the toune, £1 4s 0d
>
> Item, four foddom towes [ropes] for tyeing them and for the tawes £0 6s 8d.

The presence of the town Officers confirms the public nature of the punishment, and the need to see that matters proceeded in orderly fashion. In 1693 we find a similar entry:

> Item, to the staffman for scourging Elspeth McLauchlaue and Jonet Robertson – £1 4s 0d
>
> Item, to the officers going throw and guarding – £0 12s 0d

In another case, from May 1698, the Officers and Staffman are paid £1 4s for 'scourging a dragoun's wife who stole Charles Crysties bear'. The vagaries of seventeenth-century Scottish spelling combined with the odd menagerie of pets kept by travelling soldiers of this era make it by no means certain whether Master Crystie's loss was alcoholic or ursine in nature.

Vagabonds and Wastrels

Scourging was also the first and most frequent punishment for beggars. Desperation, hunger or despair were rarely a defence: theft was theft, and mitigating circumstances rarely a consideration. Men, women and children might be scourged, though with different degrees of severity. Eleven-year-old James Watson was taken for lifting merchant William Gilchrist's pocket book, in July 1757. His youth – and his having been detained for six weeks within the stinking and unsanitary Tolbooth during the height of summer – inclined the Bailies to release the brat and expel him from the town, with the grim rejoinder that should he ever return he would:

> Be again committed to the workhouse at hard labour for the space of 3 months and publicly whipped through the town of Stirling by the hands of the common hangman the first Friday of each month.

That, despite his youth, young Master Watson, whose tale is one of many recorded in *The Vagabond Book of Stirling* – a fascinating hand-written text detailing a miscellany of crimes, mishaps and misdemeanours within Stirling between 1752 and 1787 – should be threatened with scourging should be no surprise: he was a 'son o' the rock', after all – a local, and *known* to locals – and any punishment he received should surely reinforce local law and the security of the commonwealth. In some

Disorderly women: those women who did not display the required standards of demure, and obedient domestication were particularly prone to public punishment. From a 'Medieval Market' in Broad Street in 1994. (Photo by James Wigglesworth)

cases, though, even within this brutal era, some small mercy *was* to be found – as an entry from Christmas 1690, detailing the case of an unnamed and starving waif taken for theft on the bitter December streets, demonstrates:

> Item, to the officers for putting a young vagabond child out of toune that was taken with a stolen pan and had stolen some flesh – £0 12s 0d
> Item, payed for bread and drink to the said child a night in prison – £0 2s 0d

A night's shelter and food in his belly – well, it *was* Christmas after all – then out onto the cold and lonely winter wastes beyond the Burgh gate. Most vagrants though could not rely on a such a reception. Only a few days after the Bailies' act of festive favour we find another entry, from 9 January 1691:

> Item, to the town officers, by the magistrates order, for putting ane vagabond woman out of the town that was following the soldiers – £0 12s 0d

Camp followers condemned for 'whoredom' were sharply shown the door – or, rather, the Gate. Vagabonds or outsiders guilty of theft were treated far more harshly than *domestic* miscreants. From 6 May 1693 we find mention of 18s paid 'to the executioner for burning and scurdging [*sic*] of a vagabond named Mary Campbell'. Branding – usually on the face or shoulder – added an extra element to punishment in cases of theft, that of *recognition*. Such miscreants were, literally, *marked men* (and women), who might be easily identified and denied entry through the Barras Yett should they be foolish enough to return. Beggars, particularly, were unwelcome, and travellers could expect little but the undisguised scorn of the citizens: gathered up, roped, and bundled out of town as soon as their presence was detected. Suspicion of the outsider ensured that their being guilty of no apparent crime or criminal intent was incidental to punishment. Paranoid fear of stranger-danger is not unique to the modern era. Their treatment is often quite indistinguishable from that meted out to convicted thieves. In the summer of 1656 we find:

> Item, payit for rope to bind the Egyptians – £0 2s 8d
> Item, to the Hangman to go throw with them – £1 10s 0d

Roped, flogged and dragged through the streets of the Burgh, the *Egyptians* – as gypsies were known – would hopefully take the hint and decline from stopping off in Stirling the next time their travels brought them in this direction. No welcome, and certainly no charity was to be found here.

This is, of course, a common feature of gated or enclosed communities. As Marie Brammeld rightly observes in notes accompanying her 2010 collection of selections from *The Vagabond Book*, 'parishes looked for any opportunity they could to avoid the responsibility of paying out to the "undeserving poor", and in Stirling "deserving" meant "local"'. Some relief *was* available from charitable concerns, but these were parochial. The parish looked after its own. *Spittal's Trust*, founded by Robert Spittal, tailor to King James IV, had been offering assistance to members of the *Seven Incorporated Trades* who had fallen upon hard times since 1550, and *Allan's Mortification*, set up by lawyer John Allan in 1724, strove to attend to the education welfare of their children. *Cowane's Hospital*, established by a bequest from Stirling's greatest benefactor, John Cowane, for the maintenance of 'decayed Guild brethren' (members of the *Merchants' Guild*), had been offering aid since 1637. The *Cowane* and *Spittal Trusts*, incidentally, continue their good works to the present day. For everyone outside this *closed-shop* of mercantile mercy there was the vague hope of Poor Relief, from the kirk or the Burgh – so long as they could demonstrate that their plight was genuine, not 'of their own making', and that they were established citizens of Stirling. Brammeld highlights the case of one Jean Luckieson, from 10 March 1759:

> [Luckisson] declares that she lived in Russkie in Menteith from infancy until Martinmas last when she came to this place and took a place in John Dollar's house, and has subsisted not so much from her own labour as from what her children procured her. The Bailies consider her notorious bad character and ill house kept by her and that she has not resided in this parish for three years and so has not by law acquired any title to be burdensome.

Pauper's plight: local tradesmen and merchants could rely on charity from the Cowane and Spittal hospitals, started by local burgesses. Others were not so lucky. (Photo by David Kinnaird)

Jean's character may well have been *bad* and her house disorderly – the same entry records that her daughter, Mary Graham, was sentenced to six weeks in the Workhouse and subsequent banishment from the Burgh as a lewd 'nuisance to society' – but the point here, and its one the unknown author of *The Vagabond Book* makes every effort to hammer home, is that Luckieson is an *outsider*. She is not 'by law' entitled to be 'burdensome'. Those who *could* prove such 'title' might apply for one of a handful of official Beggar's Badges issued by the Bailies. By 1744 there were forty of these, though the dire straits resulting from a succession of pitiful harvests in the latter years of the century – along with the huge numbers of Highlanders displaced by the decimation of communities in the wake of the Jacobite defeat, and agricultural workers later left homeless by the Highland Clearances – required that a further 200 be ordered. One local clergyman complaining that the greater number of those seeking relief from the town 'are obviously of Gaelic extraction' – Gaelic implying Catholic – a sectarian resentment that would grow immensely as a consequence of the influx of Irish to the area, caused by *an Gorta Mor* – the Potato Famine of 1740-41 – during which time the rural Raploch would be derisively nicknamed 'Little Ireland'. A similar pattern is evident a century earlier, also as a result of famine, as the number of vagrants expelled from the town – an average of four a year for most of the seventeenth century – leaps to an alarming ninety in 1699. Craig Mair estimates, in *Stirling: The Royal Burgh* (1990), that around a twelfth of the local population was receiving some manner of financial support at this time. The message was clear: Stirling looked after its own, and no other.

The Workhouse

From the end of the sixteenth century, legislation in Scotland had made the Parish rather than the Church primarily responsible for poor-relief, supported in part by the *Buttock Mail*, a Poor Law tax levied as a fine for infidelity and intercourse out of wedlock ('buttock' being a common Scots euphemism for a prostitute; *mail* – as in *blackmail* – monies paid).

From 1672, when an Act was passed requiring all Burghs in Scotland to establish a House of Correction – more commonly termed the *Workhouse* – within which those deemed unable to work or provide for themselves, might be detained and set to work for the benefit of the town. From the early eighteenth century those – mostly women – who had committed minor crimes against public order or public decency would also (as we shall shortly see) frequently find themselves detained within its walls, 'there to be remain until liberated in due course of law'. This muddying of degradation and desperation – of the genuinely needy and those who were seen somehow to have disgraced their community – served to increase the stigma of incarceration for all concerned. To serve time here was no less shameful than to endure many of the public exhibitions of punishment detailed in this chapter, and the physical strains – hand-loom weaving, picking oakum (painstakingly stripping fibres of tarred rope and cordage to provide packing or 'caulking', for the joints of wooden sailing vessels) and breaking rocks – were often considerably greater. Indeed in terms of hardship the principal distinction between imprisonment within the Tolbooth and a spell in the Workhouse was that in the latter those imprisoned were fed.

The location of the original Workhouse is unknown, and a number of vacant properties appear to have been appropriated as suitable hosts over the years. John W. Small in *The Ludgings of the Earl of Mar* (1905), notes that the town council made arrangements with Lord Grange, the then owner, to convert the derelict sixteenth-century townhouse of the Earl of Mar into the Burgh Workhouse in the 1730s, dating its current title, Mar's Wark (as in *Work* – as opposed to its earlier name, Mar's *Ludging* from this period. According to Small it remained in use until the Jacobite Rebellion of 1745-46. The Ludging's famously ruinous

Picking oakum: a common occupation for
those confined within the Burgh Workhouse
and, later, the new County Jail. (Photo by David
Kinnaird, courtesy of Stirling District Tourism)

From palace to workhouse: various vacant buildings were appropriated for use as the Burgh's House
of Correction, including the former palace of the sixteenth-century Earl of Mar, John Erskine.
(Photo by David Kinnaird)

state owes more to the folly of the Young Pretender's lieutenant, Mirabel de Gordon, positioning rebel guns atop its roof – in clear line of sight of the castle's rather more formidable firepower – than it does to persistent prophetic tales of dire sixteenth-century curses placed upon the Mars by the outraged Abbot of Cambuskenneth (a fuller account of this spurious snippet of local lore can be found in this author's *Haunted Stirling*). The *Wark* decimated, rooms within William Bruce's Tolbooth were then appropriated for use: Treasurer's records from 1752 ordering that 'The three laigh [low] vaults immediately to the south of the common guardroom, in each of which there is a chimney or vent, and the two high rooms in the back prison' be prepared for service, and these were still in use long after Gray's 1785 renovation. Following the *Poor Law Amendment Act* (1845), a proper Poorhouse was finally erected in Union Street in 1957 (part of which endures to the present day as the Orchard House Hospital), administered by parochial boards and supported by a Poor Rate of 1s 3d in the pound.

The Cuck Stool

The tane, less like a Knave than Fool,
Unbidden clam the high Cockstool,
And put his heid and baith his Hands
Throw Holes where the Ill-Doer stands.

Allan Ramsey, 'The Twa Cut-Purses', 1728)

Prospective felons foolish enough not to learn the lesson of being 'dungyn sairly', could expect to make the acquaintance of the Cuck Stool, or Cock-Stool – a term often confusingly applied in Scots parlance to both the stocks, usually consisting of two timbers, hinged and locked in order to secured the arms or legs of the victim, and the upright Pillory, which also held their heads (and was often employed to show and shame more notable worthies than those consigned to the beggarly stocks). The Stirling *Cuck* is of the former design. It consists of two beams, each of which is 6 foot 6 inches length, 12 inches broad and 6 inches thick. Hinges on one end allow the other to be opened, with a series of hasps and staples on the opposite end securing the device around the ankles of those unfortunate enough to be restrained therein. Resting on two wooden supports, it is a mere 10 inches from the ground, and would have required a bench or stool to seat those confined (though given the nature of the device, their comfort was hardly a consideration). Oddly, it has seven apertures – allowing for the restraint of four (or three-and-a-half) felons.

This is almost certainly the same item mentioned in accounts for 11 September 1703, during the construction of Sir William Bruce's replacement of the dilapidated Medieval Tolbooth.

> Item, payed for more skellie to the new house of the Tolbooth, carriage of a great manie deals and tries, single and double knapple, from the house to the said new wark, a longe old oaken trie for the troan and cockstoole made new; lyme, sand, and workmanship, setting up the troane in ane uther new place in the streit, the wrights helping up that troane, with uthers, and severall uther things – £92 19s 8d

The Tron itself, then located in the upper part of Market Street (modern Broad Street) is long lost, but in this entry we see – in the 'longe old oaken trie', from which both it and the Cuck were fashioned – a link, both literal and figurative, between the bustling mercantile life of the town and the administration of punishment.

Although discomfort is clearly an essential part of such confinement, the Cuck Stool, 'paynted rede' by the Provost's order, is, first and foremost, an instrument of humiliation – a very public display of shame, the object of scorn being rendered, as

Above left Endless toil: a spell in the workhouse, occupying these Mar's Wark Chambers from 1730-1746, was often more taxing than any public punishment. (Photo by David Kinnaird)

Above right The branks: the Scold's Bridle, an instrument of humiliation for troublesome or argumentative wives. (Photo by David Kinnaird)

Ramsey's verse put it, 'less like a Knave than Fool' – and one which provided the additional indignity of audience participation, as the restrained reprobate would invariably find himself an easy target for vexatious vocalisations of public scorn, along with any easily available ordure or market place muck the mob might find at hand (hence 'cuck' or 'cack' in its title). I say *himself*, as it was generally the case that the Cuck was reserved for men of the lower orders – petty thieves, unruly or disobedient servants, unlicensed beggars or vagabonds (a term freely used in the records of Stirling to describe not only itinerant travellers but pretty much anyone the authorities thought to be of questionable character). In part this was a

The Cuck Stool and Jougs: ancient tools of public punishment, on display within the Smith Art Gallery and Museum. (Photo reproduced with kind permission of the Stirling Smith Art Gallery & Museum)

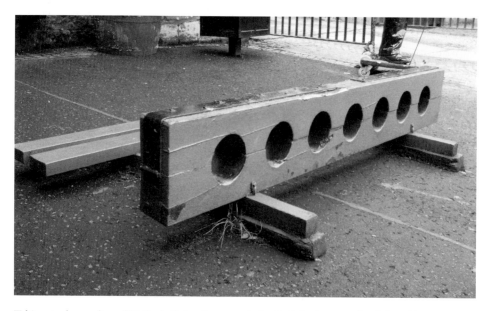

Taking stock: a replica of Stirling's distinctive seven-hole Cuck in the grounds of the Old Town Jail visitor attraction, St John Street. (Photo by David Kinnaird)

matter of *modesty*: it was simply *unseemly* to leave a woman *bare legged* and exposed. Other humiliations were available for the errant domestic drudge, who might be forced to ride through the town, their heads and shoulders immodestly uncovered on an open cart. The beldames of the Royal Burgh were clearly made of sterner stuff. John G. Harrison, in *The Stirling Tollbooth: The Building and its People 1472-1847*, is adamant that in Stirling the Cuck was exclusively a punishment reserved for women. On 26 May 1711 the council decreed that:

> An act be made for the better suppressing of the uncleanness of this place, that whatever woman shall for heirafter be found guiltie of that sin with any of the souldiers that shall happen to be quartered here, and not dilate the same to the magistrats or kirk session before the souldier guiltie with her remove from hence…[they] shall be subject to the punishment of the cockstooll and theirafter banished furth of this burgh

'Uncleanness' – the carrying of sexually transmitted diseases such as syphilis – was a greatly feared and little understood concern for communities such as Stirling: insular in so far as the population, working, living and dying within the Burgh walls were concerned, but susceptible to infections spread by travelling soldiers billeted intermittently within the castle and town, and the *camp followers* who hastened after them. The punishments meted out to such women – such as the eight 'cucked and drumed' out of town at Michelmas, 1725, following rumours that *the Pox* was rife amongst the garrison – seem incredibly harsh, and one-sided, but, as with the whipping of vagrants or vagabonds, are a primitive mechanism whereby the wellbeing and defining social compacts of a largely enclosed community might be maintained. For such women, seen by their actions (or profession) to be intrinsically immodest, there was little shame to be earned from being *Carted* through the town. For such slatterns the indignity of the *Cuck-Stool* beckoned.

Married women deemed to have challenged their natural subservient social state were also subject to severe chastisements, the most common being:

- Cowing (already mentioned), a public head-shaving, usually performed in the marketplace and reserved for those guilty of adultery – depriving wantons of the crowning glory of their hair (modest women kept their hair covered, after all).
- The Branks (Scold's Bridle), a cage fitted over the head of the argumentative wife, or 'scold', known to have challenged the authority of her husband; a sharp flange fitted into her mouth, preventing her from speaking – often at the risk of choking her or cutting her own sharp tongue; using reins attached to the Branks, the victim would be led, carted, or otherwise 'rid brankit through the toune' in seventeenth and early eighteenth-century records.

Cuckolded or bullied husbands were also chastised – dragged through the town by his peers on an open cart (a primitive variation of the 'Riding the Stang' ritual reserved for English wife-beaters of the era, who would be carried through their communities carried on a pole) in the hope that public scorn would bolster them to keep their wives under control in future.

The Jougs and Fetter-Bolts

Also in the care of the Smith Art Gallery are two other infamous instruments of restraint, the Jougs (or Juggs) and Fetter-Bolt (or Fetterlock). The former is an iron collar, the circle of its neck a snug nine inches in diameter. Two arms, 3 feet in length, extend outward from the nape of the collar, upon which two shorter extensions, hooped to serve as handcuffs, are fixed. Padlocked, the arms would then be secured to the 'bauk' (beam) of the Tron, in the market place. This Stirling Jougs dates from at least the earliest years of the eighteenth century, and is known to have been fixed to the new Tron erected in Market Street, in September 1703.

As with the Cuck, the object of this item was public humiliation, the restrained rogue required to stand upright, arms raised before them, and with their back to the mob. Such a fate was experienced by the rogue described in an entry from 1 June 1698, when the Officers and Staffman were paid a combined £1 4s for, 'standing on a theiff at the trone who stealled sheip at the Torwood'.

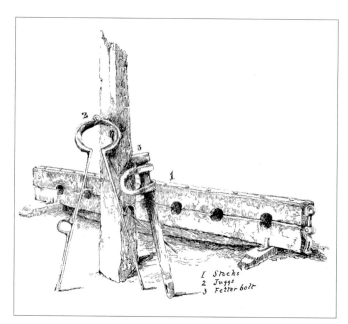

Public punishments: The Cuck Stool, Fetter-Bolt and Jougs. (Illustration by E.S. Fleming, 1898)

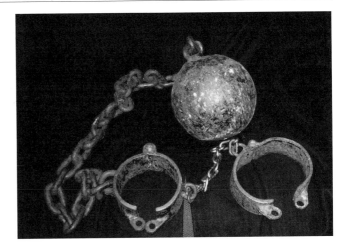

Ball and chain: shackles might be fitted around a felon's ankles – leaving him to literally carry the burden of his bondage. (Photo by David Kinnaird)

Considerably older – originally used within the 'Thieves Pot' of the sixteenth-century Bastion – is the iron Fetter-Bolt. thirty-nine inches in in length, its securing nut is some 4 inches in diameter. Designed to be fixed around one ankle only, the lock is seven inches by five, a staple-hole on one end providing a means by which the device might be secured to a wall or load-stone. A 'ponderous' instrument, in the estimation of R.S. Fleming, which simply and effectively renders its wearer immobile. This cumbersome device remained in the Bastion until at least May 1692, when records show the sum of two shillings spent 'for oyl to the irones in the thieves holl'. By the mid-eighteenth century it had been relocated to the condemned cell of the Tolbooth, remaining in regular use there until that building was taken out of service in 1847. Until recent renovations the brass hoop to which the Fetter-Bolt was locked was still firmly fixed to the floor of the chamber, its thirty-nine inches just long enough to allow the condemned prisoner a view from the cell's high window into Jail Wynd, below, where townsfolk would begin to gather for the entertainment provided by their execution in the adjacent Market Street.

Banishment – 'To forsuer the towne'

To be exiled from one's home might seem, in an age where personal mobility and freedom of movement is taken for granted, to be a soft option. For those born and bred within enclosed and self-sustaining communities such as that of the Castle Rock, it was a frightful prospect – the hostile treatment demonstrated to itinerant travellers in Stirling being typical of the reception those banished might expect elsewhere. Those possessed of a trade, or of funds sufficient to support themselves, might fare comparatively well – though few with funds or property would find themselves in such dire straits.

A prime illustration of this disparity is provided in the example of Stirling's seventeenth-century benefactor, Master John Cowane. A merchant, banker, Councillor and Dean of Guildry, as well as Commissioner to the Scots Parliament, Cowane's reputation is carried into the present day by his bequest of 40,000 Scots Merks (approximately £2,222 Sterling) in establishing Cowane's Hospital, an almshouse to provide for the 'succour of 12 decayed Gildbrothers'. Constructed between 1637 and 1649 (curtailed twice by 'visitations' of the plague), it remains an important local landmark, and a reminder of the influence (and occasional beneficence) of the local Guildry. A statue of Cowane stands proudly over the entrance. Known locally as Auld Staney Breeks – 'staney' meaning either *stone* or *stained* in the popular vernacular – it hints at the *other* reason for the Merchant's enduring notoriety, as indicated in Kirk Session Minutes for 8 August 1611:

> The quilk day compeirit Agnes Cowane, servand to Duncan Patersone and confessit fornication with John Cowane, Merchand, and that the first and last tyme was all ye monet imediatelie preceding the feast of Witsonday last. The brethrein continewis [furder] with her quile ye said Jonne be also tried.

For his sins Cowane was fined £6 (approximately £1 Sterling, at this point), and ordered to sit upon the Penance Stool before the doors of the Holy Rude church 'upon the nixt six sermon days'. John G. Harrison notes in *The World of John Cowane*

that three sittings was the standard penalty for a first-time fornicator, so John's dalliance with young Mistress Cowane (no relation, as far as we know) is likely to have been a frequent offender. He certainly doesn't seem to have learned from his costly lesson, as in 1615 an identical encounter is described in the Parish Records of Callendar, with one Christian McGibbon of Menteith. In both cases the object of the Merchant's amour was left pregnant. McGibbon's fate is not known, but it is unlikely to

Auld staney breeks: merchant John Cowane's statue stands proudly over the entrance to his hospital. He could afford to pay the price of his sins. Others involved often bore a much greater burden. (Photo by David Kinnaird)

differ from that of the unfortunate Agnes, who was also forced to sit in shame upon the Penance Stool, fined the lesser sum of £2 (a crippling sum for a serving-girl), then banished from the Burgh.

Cowane was legally obliged to support his illegitimate offspring for the first seven years of their lives, but that, of course, assumed that the banished girls and their offspring survived separation from their families. Even should an unskilled servant find employment in another household, elsewhere, their prospects remained poor. Who, after all, would welcome a known wanton within their homes – particularly one who brought the additional expense of another mouth to feed.

The penalty for flouting the authority of the courts could be severe. In early October 1758, Janet McGowan, banished from the Burgh in May the previous year, was discovered in the house of Excise Officer William Seton, in the act of purloining a pound of loose candles and a 'ling fish' (unsalted dried cod, a popular preserve of the era). Having, prior to her original expulsion from the town, been 'long committed to the workhouse for different acts of theft', the bench railed against the unrepentant jade. On 12 October the Bailie appointed her:

> ... to be again committed to the workhouse till Friday the 20th October, then carried by the Officers to the head of the forestreet and to be from thence whipped by the hands of the common Hangman attended by the officers to the Boroughs Gate, receiving the usual number of lashes upon her naked back at the usual places and thereafter renews the former sentence of banishment.

In June 1755 Bailie James Jaffray spared another unauthorised returnee, Margaret Ross, this ordeal, on 'in respect [that] she had some small children' (whether her offspring remained in their mothers care during banishment, or resided within the town, maternal yearnings perhaps accounting her risky return, is unclear), but warned that this mercy would not be extended again. If so she would '...again be commited to the workhouse at hard labour for the space of three months and publickly whipped...through the Burgh the first Friday of each month'. On the final Friday she would 'be burnt on the face and again banished'.

Such threats, though generally sufficient to deter rogues from returning, were not always effective. In order to avoid sentencing for her ill-tempered abuses of shoemaker James Lyon, Janet Bunton agreed to voluntarily banish herself, on 18 August 1763. Voluntary banishments were not uncommon, particularly for those – like Elizabeth Barclay, accused of 'behaving very indecently, and entertaining bad company', in August 1767, and the girlfriends of Town Drummer James Drummond, mentioned earlier – who wished to avoid the public shame of a trial. With the consent of the wronged party, the authorities could often be persuaded to permit such expeditious exits, if only to spare themselves the cost of public punishment.

The belligerent Bunton, however, was still in the Burgh six weeks later, having been committed to the Workhouse for 'sundry abuses' of her neighbours. She was immediately ordered to 'be conveyed by the town officers with their halberds and the drum beating to the Port of Stirling bareheaded', and promised the same 'severe certifications', detailed above, should she return. Some eleven years later she *reappears* in records, held as a possible accessory to beggar Christian McNab, who had (rather foolishly) attempted the theft and resale of bottles belonging to Provost (and 'Black Bondsman') James Alexander, and found herself swiftly shunted, alongside her erstwhile partner-in-crime, 'without the burrows gate with the Staffman going behind the said delinquents with his whip in his hand.' Undeterred, she is back again, in August 1774, at which point – clearly exasperated –

> the Baillie therefor appoints her to be recommitted to the Workhouse therein to remain till tomorrow until twelve o clock midday, and then betwixt that hour and one o clock afternoon to be carried prisoner by the Town Officers to the head of the Mercate Place at Mar's Work there to have her head and shoulder uncovered, and her arms tied behind her with a piece of rope, the end of which is to be held in the Staffman's left hand and his whip in the other and from thence appoints her to be conducted down the principle streets of the burgh in the above manner to the Burrows Gate, the officers also attending with their Halberts and the Town Drum beating behind her – and thereafter of new banishes her this Burgh and Territories thereof in all time coming with certification if she ever return she will again be committed to the Workhouse at hard labour until the first Friday after being apprehended and then publickly whipped through the Burgh by the hands of the common Hangman.

Learning the lessons of their past laxity the Bailies add that:

> so often as she may thereafter return to the Burgh ordains her to be in like manner apprehended imprisoned and publickly whipped between the hours of twelve and one the Friday next after to her being apprehended. There is no record of Janet returning again to the Burgh, but it would hardly be a surprise to anyone if she had.

It should be no surprise, by now, to learn that the vast majority of those Banished from the town – a ratio of more than 4-to-1 – were female. On 24 June 1669 the Burgh Court had decreed that no woman should be allowed – on threat of banishment – to live in a house on her own, or to rent rooms to others, who was not the widow or daughter of a burgess of the Burgh. As with so many other punitive rulings, previously discussed, this was a matter of social control. It sought to not only curtail the 'lewd practices' of would-be brothel-keepers and others deemed by their riotous behaviour to keep a 'bad house', but, for the property-owning burgesses, had a far more immediate practical purpose. 'The object of this,' John G. Harrison notes in *The World of John Cowane*, 'is to keep down wages, to ensure an adequate supply of servants, and to ensure that…they can be more readily controlled.' Although she was banished for snatching a pair of new shoes from her employer, Deacon of the Hammermen, Walter Allan, in December 1752, servant girl Martha Ferrier – who has the distinction of featuring in the very first case recorded in *The Vagabond Book of Stirling* – would have most likely endured the same penalty simply for leaving Allan's household and service without his consent.

By the latter half of the eighteenth century, banishment, often preceded by a spell in the Burgh Workhouse, but with a gradual diminution, over time, of the threat of *scourging* or branding, became the norm for any woman held to have 'given public offence by their indecent behaviour' – such as Mary Graham, recent bride of Corporal John Robison, discovered at midnight on 23 March 1759 in a bed in the Widow Farrier's house with the Sergeant of a recruiting party. Mary's excuse that she simply had not *noticed* that the Sergeant was *there* raised a few eyebrows, as there was known to be only *one* bed in the house. When James Wingate, Maltman, Brewer and the founder of Wingate's Inn – which survives to the present day as King Street's Golden Lion Hotel – testified that 'for some weeks past it was currently reported in his neighbourhood that Widow Ferrier kept a bad house and harboured soldiers and other loose company', the widow put up her shutters and fled the town. Mary Graham, already in custody for her 'lewd behaviour', was banished.

On 2 October 1757, teenage strumpet Margaret Brown was installed in the Workhouse. Her crime? That on:

> Monday forenoon she came to Bannockburn and fell into company with some of the soldiers in the town, and with 2 of the soldiers [she] drank 2 bottles of ale and a dram in the house of Mrs Whitfield… [then] in the morning of that same day she went with the soldiers to a house in the Castle Wynd where they drank about five bottles of ale, and stayed till it was late in the night, or rather early in the morning, when she and the soldiers went to a room of John Bayne's in the Mary's Wynd where the soldiers were quartered, and she passed the night with them until about 5 o'clock in the morning.

One might think that Margaret, who described herself to the Bailies as having been, 'since she was 7 years old…a coal-bearer, first in the Duke of Hamilton's coal works and for about these five years bygone in Lord Boyd's', might be entitled to a little light relief. The hefting of freshly hewn coal through the dense, dusty seams and shafts of these mines – labour usually assigned to children or younger woman on account of their small stature, was literally back-breaking work. Her behaviour was, however, 'a front to the public decency', and she might have expected more serious penalty had it not been discovered that she was not the hard-done-by collier's lass she claimed to be, but, rather, one Elizabeth Clerk, daughter of an ale-seller and a labourer at the Greenland Fishery. After three weeks in the Workhouse she too was banished.

On 5 February 1760, Janet Scott, heavily pregnant, was taken for lifting the purse and a quantity of satin ribbon from the pocket of George Morison at the Fair Day market. Her unsubtle skills as a pick-pocket leaving much to be desired, Morison reported that:

> in the market place the said woman came close to him and he found something slip out of his breech [trouser] pocket and upon examining found he had lost the purse which was a small bladder, and immediately followed the woman, and…the woman dropped the purse or bladder with a piece of narrow black satin ribbon.

It is impossible not to feel some small sympathy for the desperate Janet, abandoned spouse of William Anderson, a soldier in the Cameronian Regiment, 'lately draughted from that regiment and sent to America'. Assigned to the Workhouse, she was liberated by the magistrates a mere ten days later, 'in respect that she appears big with child', and banished. We would be in error, however, to believe that such rulings showed magisterial mercy for these pathetic examples of the fair sex, as Marie Brammeld supposes in consideration of a similar case, from December 1763 – that of petty thief Mary Miller. Miller, previously banished, fearfully ill and in obvious distress, had been apprehended almost immediately upon her return by the Officers – ever vigilant of diseases and infections which could quickly spread within enclosed and overcrowded communities. On closer consideration, however, what seems like a lenient renewal of the terms of the unfortunate woman's original expulsion, was in fact performed with the bare minimum of ritual:

> The Bailie considering that Mary Miller is at present under bodily distress, and not being able to undergo the punishment she deserves, he appoints her to be conveyed by the Town Officers to the Port [gate] of Stirling with the drum beating.

This *isn't* mercy. Rather it is a simple act of penny-pinching expedience: if Mary died in the Workhouse, the Burgh would be liable for the costs of her burial. Similarly, Janet Scott's care, and that of her expected child – or the burial of both, if the strains of hard labour proved too much during her confinement – was a burden the Bailies would be keen to avoid. What happened to these poor creatures after they departed the Barras Yett was no concern of the Bench.

By the late eighteenth century, banishment appears to be the preferred court-appointed punishment for petty theft and public disorder offences, too. Along with 'committal at labour' to the public Workhouse, it is the most common penalty recorded in *The Vagabond Book*. In January 1764, John McDougal, a former soldier in Major McLean's Battalion of Foot, was expelled for verbally abusing Collector of Excise James Dunbar and threateningly 'lurking in the Collector's close under cloud of night'. The nature of their dispute is not recorded, though animosity for the tax man was as common in the 1760s as it is today. Alexander Noble's purchase of purloined firearms from a soldier in the castle stores saw him similarly expelled, in May 1775.

'Resurrection Men'

Banishment, in at least one famous instance, proved to be the only verdict legally available to the Bailies. On 19 November 1822 a middle-aged matron of the town, Mary Witherspoon, was buried in the Holy Rude kirkyard. Three days later, her mortal remains were disinterred and sold for £10 to local medical student John Forrest for anatomical study and dissection. The culprits were quickly identified: former schoolmaster Daniel Mitchell, and the church Sexton, James McNab – who had himself buried Mary. Forrest fled, disposing of the body before he departed – and causing two immediate problems for the Court.

Firstly, it was required that the charges against the grave robbers be re-drafted. During this delay the pair were released from the Tolbooth by their drunken jailor, prompting their outraged neighbours – armed with stones, sticks and cudgels – to assault McNab in his lodgings, and to pursue his panicked partner across the rooftops of the Old Town. Soon both were securely in the cells once more, though their safety was by no means assured. The mob were beginning to converge on Jail Wynd, and the panicked Provost reluctantly called upon the castle garrison for aid. One anxious soldier discharged a warning shot over their heads, prompting a riot – the townsfolks' sticks and stones clashing against the soldiers' bayonets and rifle-butts. Miraculously, no fatalities resulted. A more serious issue however, and one which posed a serious challenge to the authorities, eager to regain order in the town and placate the anguished and angry citizens, was how to deal with the villains now in their care. Under Scots law, a dead body had no value, and in the absence of reliable witnesses or proof of theft – grave clothes or other identifiable items stolen from the corpse – a successful prosecution was unlikely. Only a few years later Edinburgh's rather more infamous body-snatchers, Burke and Hare, would be unsuccessfully tried for the many crimes perpetrated in supplying that city's anatomists with fresh flesh. Unable to find material evidence of their mercenary, murderous endeavours – the corpses having been burned, buried or otherwise rendered unidentifiable by anxious physicians eager to conceal their complicity – William Burke was finally prosecuted for the lesser offence of *theft*, having been found in possession of a shawl belonging to one victim. Even then, William Hare escaped prosecution, having

Victim of the Resurrectionists –
Mary Witherspoon was the only
known victim of Stirling's own
'body-snatchers', Mitchell and
McNab, in 1923. (Photo by Patricia
Brannigan)

An ironic end: body-snatcher Billy
Burke was publicly dissected after
his execution in 1829. This portion
of his skin was donated to a local
museum by a Bridge of Allen
physician in 1890. Burke's wife,
Stirling woman Helen M'Dougal,
was beaten to death by an angry
mob soon after her return to the
area. (Photo reproduced by kind
permission of the Stirling Smith
Art Gallery and Museum)

been persuaded to turn King's Evidence against his partner, as the only witness to his wrongdoing. Burke's hanging, in the city's Grassmarket on 28 January 1829, and his subsequent dissection by local surgeons (the gallows being one of the few *legal* sources of surgical specimens, prior to the *Anatomy Act* of 1832), went some small way to placate the blood-crazed mob. No material evidence linked the sexton and the schoolmaster to the posthumous fate of Widow Witherspoon. Only one option was available if the threat of further public outrage was to be averted. They were banished. Armed guards continued to patrol the churchyard by night for many months, and a watchtower was erected near John Cowane's Hospital, but no similar cases of are recorded in the Burgh records.

The instigator of their wrongdoing, John Forrest – part of a long established line of burgesses – did eventually return to Stirling, after long service as an army surgeon. He soon enjoyed elevation to the post of Inspector-General of Hospitals for Scotland. He was never prosecuted. Helen M'Dougal, widow of William Burke – portions of whose remains were sold off at public auction following his dissection (one such was donated to the Smith Art Gallery and Museum in 1890 by Bridge of Allan physician and antiquary Dr Alex Paterson) – had family in Stirling, and returned to the district following her husband's execution, no doubt to escape the wrath of her Edinburgh neighbours, suspicious of her apparent complicity in the 'body-snatchers' deadly trade. It was to be a short stay. Only three days after she started work at Perth's Deanstone Cotton Mill, her past caught up with her. A luridly titled Glasgow Broadside, *An Account of the Horrid and Barbarous Murder of Helen M'Dougal, Wife of the Miscreant BURKE*, dated 25 April 1829, tells of how she was done to death 'by a great number of Individuals, most of them Females, who attacked her furiously, siezed her by the hair of the head and strangled her, one of the women dispatched her by putting her foot on her breast, and crushed her severely.'

Transportation –'To His Majesty's Colonies'

Returning to matters of theft, *The Vagabond Book* records – in entries for July and August 1752 – the case of drover John McMartin, who had brought cattle to the Stirling market from Gallachie, north-east of Inverness. After a reckless night carousing in the local taverns, McMartin was taken by the Town Officers for lifting 'six folding knives and…two dozen yellow metal buttons' from a local trader. Closer inspection revealed a more impressive haul, liberated from others selling their wares amongst the huddle of makeshift wooden booths cluttering Market Street, comprising, '6 bone combs, garter strings, 6 pairs of stockings, 3 blue bonnets, 4 and a half yards of tartan plaid and a piece of white cloth out of George Graham, Chapman'. It appears to have been this vigilant vendor (a Chapman being, essentially, an itinerant vendor – or travelling-salesman) who noticed the drover's spree amongst the stalls and raised the alarm. As an outsider, if tried for theft, McMartin might be hanged. At best a conviction could see him branded or lugged. After six weeks sweltering in the stinking cells of the Tolbooth, however, another alternative presented itself:

> The said John McMartin to avoid a trial for the crimes foresaid hereby voluntarily banishes himself from the Kingdom of Scotland in all time coming during his lifetime…

Liberty, albeit on foreign soil? Not quite. The entry continues, thus:

> William McAdam, Burgess of Glasgow for and in the name of William Lary, shipmaster…hereby enacts himself to transport the said John McMartin to one or other of His Majesty's plantations in America, and to report a certificate from the proper officer of having landed him there under the penalty of 20 pounds in case of failzie [failure].

So, not simply banishment, but *transportation* to the Americas: penal servitude within the cotton and tobacco fields. Slavery, essentially. This punishment had been available to most British courts since the earliest years of the seventeenth century, though it does not appear to have been a popular penalty in Scotland (much less so in Stirling) until the middle of the eighteenth, largely on account of the feudal, local nature of much Scots justice prior to the *Heritable Jurisdictions Act*, mentioned earlier. In 1720 an extension of the *Piracy Act* (1717) (its breathless full title, 'An Act for the further preventing Robbery, Burglary, and other Felonies, and for the more effectual Transportation of Felons, and unlawful Exporters of Wool; and for Declaring the Law upon some Points relating to Pirates'), authorised payments by the state to those tasked to deliver convicts to the colonies. One such was Glasgow merchant and ship-owner, William McAdam. It is perhaps a small mercy that McMartin was not burdened, like so many before him, with the cost of paying his own passage into penal servitude. In the Plantations, he might be fortunate to meet a few familiar faces, many captive Highlanders (those rebels who had escaped the slaughter perpetrated by '*Butcher Cumberland*', Prince William, Duke of Cumberland, son of King George II) having been sold into slavery there in the aftermath of the Jacobite defeat at Drumossie Moor (Culloden), on 16 April 1746.

Incidentally, one of the most popular contemporary accounts of the Jacobites' fall, the epic verse 'A History of the Rebellion'(1753), was the work of the 'hunchback' poet, Dugald Graham, born in the Raploch area of Stirling, and – like George Graham (no relation, as far as this author can determine) who brought the drover's crimes to light – a Chapman. McMartin made a serious error in stealing

The Mercat Cross: repeat offenders might have their ears nailed to the public scales, the Tron, by the Mercat Cross – then cut off and left on display as a bloody deterrent to others. (Photo by David Kinnaird)

from members of this profession. Although by no means men of high status – in the eyes of many Bailies they were little better than Tinkers, touting their services door-to-door – they were the news-vendors of the day. Their *chapbooks'* – small, self-published pamphlets, mixing myth, whimsy, ballad lyrics, and almanacs of crime and punishment, as well as accounts of news and current affairs – were the popular periodicals of their day. Either in print, or through the wildfire of market gossip, news of John McMartin's shame, particularly if taken to trial, would soon spread far and wide.

Another voluntary lifetime banishment 'to St Christopher's or other of His Majesties colonies beyond the seas' is recorded for Margaret Stewart in 1759. Margaret, a maidservant, denied the charge of 'child-murder' for which she had been imprisoned, but declared that 'even the imputation of it' would make her life in the area intolerable. Transportation was preferable to the shame and ordeal of trial. Arrangements were made for her departure on *The Pill*, moored at Greenock.

Chillingly, transportation may not have been the only form of slavery to which felons in eighteenth-century Scotland might be sentenced. An engraved brass collar in the Museum of Scotland bears the grim message 'Alexr Stewart found guilty of death for theft at Perth the 5 December 1701 and gifted as a perpetual servant to Sir John Erskine of Alva'. Dredged from the River Forth, its wearer is presumed to have drowned while trying to escape. Although no records remain of such punishment being enacted by the Burgh's Bailies, Stewart's *Master*, the Laird of Alva, is known to have many close Stirling connections.

Between 1790 and 1855 there is a dramatic increase in instances of transportation as a sentence of the Stirling Courts, even for crimes of petty larceny, which might previously have earned villains a short spell in the Workhouse, or exclusion from the town. A brief review of those incarcerated in the cells of the new County Jail on 31 March 1851, shows a number of prisoners awaiting transportation: Margaret McLaughlin, sentenced to one years' penal servitude in the Australian colonies for lifting a watch; Mary Rankine, seven years for theft; Mary Lockhart, the same, for stealing pillow cases; Margaret Clements, seven years for lifting a petticoat; seven more for sailor Alexander McKenzie, transported for making off with a hen; baker John Russell and iron worker Joseph McConnell, each sentenced to seven years for their part in the theft of 100 fathoms of rope. It is interesting to note that nineteen-year-old Belfast soldier Daniel Quin was to be incarcerated for a mere twelve months for a serious assault on two local women, and porter John Roy and collier John McGovan, also guilty of violent affray, are given four months and thirty days respectively (to put this in perspective, collier brothers Robert and Walter Hoggans were detained for *three months* for theft of *potatoes*). It may be a little too simplistic to assume that such sentencing arises merely from greater importance being assigned to crimes against property than those against the person – though this, certainly, is often true. The reasons for the majority of Stirling's transportees during this period being female is far more insidious. Then (as now) women enjoy greater stamina and longevity: older or widowed women were considered amongst those most likely to become burdensome to the parish. It was better, therefore, that – should the opportunity to dispose of that responsibility avail itself – such women be disposed of while they still have a few years labour in them (Lockhart, Rankine and Clements were forty-one, forty-six and fifty-two respectively), ridding the Burgh of responsibility. Their sentence completed, prisoners might be granted a *Free Pass* (or *Pardon*) or *Conditional Pass*. The former was uncommon, and, if granted, would allow the parolee to return home, so long as they could pay their own passage. The latter left former prisoners free to go anywhere they chose, on the *condition* that it was *not* back to Britain. Thirty-six-year-old Margaret McLaughlin's one-year sentence might seem relatively lenient compared to others noted here – but whatever her fate she was unlikely to be permitted legally to return to

Staffman's tool: an eighteenth-century clasp knife, of the
sort used by the Stirling Staffman in lugging his victims.
(Image courtesy of James Nunn)

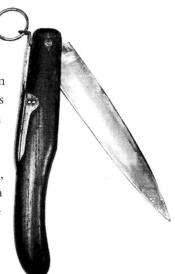

her home and husband in Stirling. Transportation
of notably violent offenders, such as Quin, was
comparatively rare, for the very simple reason
that they posed a palpable threat to the discipline
of such settlements and a potentially dangerous
challenge to the authority of guards and overseers,
often responsible for the supervision of as many as a
hundred convicts at a time. The last prisoner to be
transported from Stirling was in 1867.

Lugging

On 17 December 1546, John Fisher confessed to a catalogue of petty larceny.
From Thomas Millar's purse he took twenty-eight shillings – more than enough, in
itself, to ensure his hanging, according to the criteria noted in the *Fragmenta Collecta*;
from James McKeson he stole clothing; and from Bessie Smith three cakes, malt, a
baked chicken, and a basket in which to stow his stash. Whether Master Millar enjoyed
the favour of the Bailies is a matter of opinion: he was somehow spared the gallows,
but was sentenced to have his ear nailed to the Tron, then cut off by the Staffman –
the severed *lug* (ear) being left displayed on the *bauk* as a deterrent to other larcenous
louts. Millar was then branded upon the cheek, and scourged through the town to
the accompaniment of the Town Drum – banished from the Burgh on pain of death.
An almost identical fate was shared by thieves in an entry for 14 October 1699:

> Item, to the four officers convoying Robert and John Alders and John Spaden to the
> Gallous, where tuo of their lugs were cut out and they burnt on the brow – £3 6s od

Luggings – for which purpose the Staffman was provided with his distinctive
clasp-knife – were by no means as common in Stirling's history as are popularly
believed. Certainly, they occur with considerably lesser frequency than other
recorded physical punishments. Aside from the related risks of infection and illness,
lugging – like branding – provided a *permanent* humiliation, particularly when
combined with the double-whammy of banishment. Wherever a *lugged* felon went
he would be known as a thief and, most likely, denied entry on precisely those
grounds from gated communities like that from which he had been expelled.

Whether due to the effectiveness of this punishment as a deterrent or to a growing distaste for such visceral acts of public vengeance, luggings were rare enough by 1722 for the town treasurer to be irked by a request from the Staffman for the three shillings required to purchase a *new* knife with which to cut off the ear of an unfortunate lady named Catherine McNab.

Hanging

The standard method of punishment for the most serious of civic crimes – murder, robbery with violence and forgery – hanging was, again, less readily employed in Stirling than might be assumed. Here, as John G. Harrison observes, 'there was no question of death for stealing a loaf.' There are exceptions to this rule, of course. On 24 April 1525:

> Ritschart Broun was convictit and filit for the thyftuis steilling of twa maris [mares] out of the landis of Corntoun, and thereafter that the doume was giftin of him to be hangit quhill he war deid, he grantit of his awin fre will that he staw ane mair fra Robe Lam and ane black horse out of the Cobiltoun.

Hangman's Entry: overgrown and bricked-up, the doorway through which prisoners might be marched to their execution at the Gallows Mauling can still be found on the Back Walk. (Photo by David Kinnaird)

Broad Street: with the fall of the Burgh Gates, executions were relocated to the busy Market Street, now Broad Street. (Photo by David Kinnaird)

Occasional hangings for theft – usually of horses and livestock – *do* appear in the historical record covering the following three centuries, but with increasing rarity, and usually in cases where attendant violence has occurred. In Stirling there were very practical reasons for this, foremost amongst which was the simple fact that the original gibbet used at the *Gallows Mailing* had to be set up especially for each occasion. The Treasurer's accounts for 1689 record several instances of eight shillings paid that year 'fore careing upe ane dounthe kirk lethers', a further ten for its assembly and dismantlement, not to mention the costs – detailed elsewhere – incurred in *staffing* each execution. Originally the condemned would be escorted by the Staffman and Town Officers from the Tolbooth then, his arms bound, slowly drummed through an archway in the Burgh Wall known as the Hangman's Entry – long since bricked-up, but still visible. From thence the executioner's entourage would lead him along the Back Walk to the *Mailing*, beyond the Barras Yett.

The original Gib was little more than a ladder to be pushed away from a free-standing frame. Slow strangulation would follow, along with the humiliation of the anxious and involuntary evacuation of bowels (and, for men, the peculiar priapic consequence of gradual asphyxia which helped coin the term 'well hung'). Women, in small consideration of their modesty, had their skirts tied about their ankles. A slow and painful ordeal, it was, very occasionally, survivable.

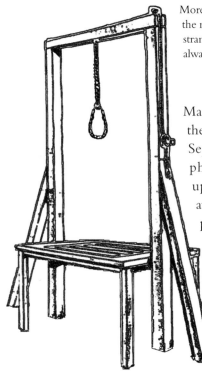

More humane? A sudden drop through a trap-door would snap the neck of the condemned, offering a swifter end than slow strangulation on the traditional Gib. In Stirling, things didn't always go according to plan. (Illustration by David Kinnaird)

Maggie Dickson was hanged for child-murder at the Common Gib at Edinburgh's Grassmarket in September 1742. Declared dead by the attending physician, she startled onlookers by bolting upright as her *corpse* was about to be carried away. The authorities were unable to repeat her punishment: Maggie was *legally* dead – and had a notarised death certificate to prove it. Auld Reekie's most infamous rogue, Councillor-cum-Housebreaker Deacon William Brodie, had fashioned Scotland's first drop-gallows in 1788 – a modern gibbet, upon which the noosed neck of the condemned was snapped by a short, sharp drop through a trap-door – and was, ironically, the first villain to be despatched upon it. A myth persists that he survived, a protective silver tube having been placed in his windpipe by an obliging French physician. True or not, while such a device might well inhibit strangulation on the old tilting-frame, and slightly increase the condemned's prospects of survival, it would *not* prevent his neck from snapping.

Unsurprisingly, there are *no* reports of such survivals in the Stirling records. The desperate events following the execution of teenage housebreaker John Campbell, executed on 14 May 1824 – on the rather more effective drop-gallows, which had finally made its first appearance in Market Street in October 1811, with the despatch of the equally burglarious Robert Brown Anderson and James Menzies – do, however, have odd echoes of Brodie's end. A feeble-minded child, Campbell was a pathetic figure. Upon being sentenced his wailing and cries for pity, according to the contemporary broadside account of his tale, caused 'general distress' amongst the population. He is described as:

...breaking out into the most heart-rending lamentations, and otherwise exhibiting such a want of fortitude,—that many were led to conjecture that there was at least a temporary destitution of reason...His conduct continued nearly the same long after he was taken out of Court, and for several days after his condemnation, the cries from his cell arrested and annoyed the passengers on the streets.

His youth and apparent feebleness of mind might have earned Campbell 'the extension of Royal Mercy' had he not (like so many others before him) briefly escaped from the Tolbooth. Even so, it was 'deemed necessary to attend him constantly, both with the view of keeping him more at ease, and of preventing the sentence of the law from being self-anticipated'. As his last dawn approached Campbell surprised onlookers by displaying *'a great degree of fortitude'*, as he was attended by the local clergy – an obligation placed upon them by the courts, not only to provide succour for the condemned, but to encourage as vocal a display of public penitence as possible. Shortly before 2 p.m. he was led into the courtroom, and further 'religious exercises' were performed. Finally, attended by the Revd Mr Anderson of Blairlogie, he moved forward to the scaffold. As the bolt to open the trap-door was opened the desperate teenager lost his new-found nerve: he 'seized the rope with his hand, and…by injuring the fall, prolonged his agony for some time.'

In struggling the simple-minded boy inhibited the drop that would have snapped his neck and instantly ended his misery. Instead he was left flailing, utterly terrified, as the breath was crushed from him. The introductory paragraph of the broadside relating the details of Campbell's demise promises an account of 'his affecting farewell with his aged Father', but fails to fulfil this obligation. John Campbell Snr, though, still had a ghoulish part to play in his son's tawdry tale. Having been convinced by an unscrupulous St Ninians physician that the boy could be revived by means of medicinal blood-letting, he hurried his heir's corpse away from the gallows. The lad's neck unbroken, there is a remote prospect that the peculiar device said to have been employed by Deacon Brodie might *possibly* have aided such industrious reanimation. Blood-letting and mercenary quackery, as John's broken-hearted father would soon discover, would *not*.

If the Broadside's description of Campbell's end sounds like a melodramatic precursor to the finale of Michael Curtiz's classic Warner Bros gangster fable *Angels With Dirty Faces* (1938), we should not be surprised. It was as dramatically satisfying (if morally simplistic) in 1824 for a villain to be suddenly stricken with a guilty conscience as it would be when Jimmy Cagney and Pat O'Brien went head-to-head on the silver screen. It's no far cry from Campbell's reported 'How will I be able to suffer such a death?' to Cagney's 'Oh please! I don't want to burn in Hell!' Like public punishments themselves, the broadsides served to conspicuously demonstrate not only that justice was seen to be done, but that the wantons and wastrels they described had, at last, seen the error of their wicked ways. Campbell's anxieties ceased, we are told, 'while conversing with religious people' and he 'frequently stated that his hope rested solely on the merits of our Saviour'. The account of debauchery and repentance apparently given by twenty-three-year-old burglar William Taylor, hanged in 1790 – and, curiously, the only felon executed in

Public repentance: an artist's rendering of William Taylor's 'Confession and Dying Declaration'. It was expected that the condemned make a show of public penitence.

Stirling during this era *not* listed in Alex Young's *Encyclopaedia of Scottish Executions: 1750–1963* (1998) – goes much further. He expounds with almost evangelical zeal of his origins: born of 'honest and creditable Parents who gave me an education suitable to their circumstances, and gave good and wholesome instructions, training me up in the ways of virtue and religion' confessing that 'in short, had I followed their counsels and advices, I would not have come to this untimely and shameful death'*;* abandoning his apprenticeship as a nail-maker he says, 'I thought…a burden taken off me, and that I was at liberty to do any thing when I was rid of my Masters superintendency'; he regales his audience with the sordid details of his fall into vice, theft and, worst of all, blaspheming, and 'horrid to think, calling upon His name for damnation to my soul'. As a salutary lesson to other like-minded apprentice-boys inclined to a life of risk and criminal romance, he concludes (with rather more poetry than might have been predicted from a burglar) that his sins are 'more in number than the sand upon the sea shore'*,* and that he is 'shortly to appear before Almighty God to answer for these, my numberless transgressions'. This eloquent epistle on the virtues of familial, civic and religious responsibility is made all the *more* remarkable when one discovers that he was completely illiterate. To those that purchased such a *'Confession and Dying Declaration'*, *actual* truth was of little import. What mattered was that conspicuous repentance reinforced social standards – preferably accompanied by plenty of juicy details of their dastardly doings.

The Last Man

In the two decades following Campbell's hanging there were only *five* executions in Stirling – one (John McGraddy, 1826) for aggravated house-breaking, and four (Peter Moffat, 1826; Robert Tennant, 1833; Alexander Millar, 1837; and Allan Mair, 1843) for murder. The last of these was also the final public execution in the Burgh.

Mair, an eighty-four-year-old farmer from Candie End, also has the distinction of being the oldest man to be executed in Great Britain during the whole of the nineteenth century. A foul tempered bully, he had beaten to death his wife of thirty years, Mary Fletcher, 86. Following her death, on 14 May 1842, neighbours were quick to testify as to the many cruelties suffered by the poor creature: she was burned, beaten, starved and locked in a trunk for hours at a time – her only comfort coming from the kindness of neighbours who would sneak into Mair's home while he was in town to feed her beef tea. Modern readers might wonder why these good neighbours did not demonstrate the greater kindness of intervening, and reporting his abuse to the Bailies. The simple and unpleasant truth of the matter is that it was entirely *legal* to beat one's wife: some, indeed, saw it as a husband's *duty* in ensuring domestic harmony.

Blaming his every misfortune on 'bloody Mary', and on a conspiracy against him by his neighbours, Mair was pronounced guilty, and cast into the Tolbooth's condemned cell (now a stationary cupboard), where his aged ankle was fixed with a brass hoop to the flagstone floor by the rather *more* ancient Fetter-Bolt. It had been five years since the previous hanging in Market Street (now becoming better known as the *Broad Street*) and the hope of the penny-pinching Bailies and Councillors was that the farmer's infirmity, combined with the dire conditions evident within the jail – it having been officially declared 'the worst jail in Britain' by newly-appointed Inspector of Prisons, Frederick Hill, that very year – would save the town the expense of hiring a hangman to end his life. They were to be disappointed. Even the prospect that, like Campbell, he might 'self-anticipate' the sentence of the courts – ending his life through hunger-strike – was short-lived: as one broadside of the day put it, 'the cravings of nature became too much to withstand, and he afterwards partook of his victuals freely' – his newfound appetite providing the local gossips with far greater *proof* of his guilt than his grumbling refusal of the counsel of clergy.

The body in the box: the last remains of murderer Allan Mair, buried beneath this pend in 1843, were rediscovered during renovations of the Tolbooth in 2000. (Photo by David Kinnaird)

Go down, Moses! The face of the Lawgiver looks out from the side entrance to the Tolbooth's courtroom. The uppermost window visible is the condemned cell – now a stationary cupboard. (Photo by David Kinnaird)

Last man hanged: the spirit of Allan Mair (author David Kinnaird), the last man publicly hanged in Stirling, is said to haunt his former prison, and makes regular visitations on the Stirling GhostWalk. (Photo by Bonnie Nicolson)

Finally, on Wednesday, 4 October 1843, after eighteen months' incarceration, he was carried to the scaffold. Too feeble to stand or to otherwise resist, he was loosely bound to the stool upon which he had sat to enjoy his final meal. Alex Young draws on contemporary newspaper accounts of Alan's final moments. '[His] whole appearance indicating the utmost degree of human frailty, borne down by the intense idea of grief', he begged the Bailies grace to address the crowd. No doubt expecting something in the manner of William Taylor's woeful self-flagellation, they were again to be sorely disappointed. Drysdale give a colourful account of this last oration:

The meenister o' the parish invented lies against me. Folks, yin an' a, mind I'm nae murderer. I ne'er committed murder, an' I say as a dyin' man who is about to pass into the presence of his Goad, I was condemned by the lees o' the minister, by the injustice o' the Sheriff and Fiscal, and perjury of the witnesses. I trust for their conduct that a' thae parties shall be overta'en by the vengeance of Goad, and sent intae everlasting damnation. I curse them with the curses in the Hunner and Ninth Psalm – 'Set thou a wicked man o'er them' – an' haud on thee, hangman, till I'm dune – 'An' let Satan stand at thyeir right haun. Let their days be few, let their children be faitherless, let their weans be continually vagabonds…'

After a few minutes of this splenetic onslaught, neither the crowd nor Glasgow hangman John Murdoch was inclined to 'haud on'. The bolt was pulled. In mid rant – the appropriately dramatic 'I curse them a…' – Mair dropped. Here the farmer's final fate takes on much of the unsettling character of Jamie Campbell's last moments. Somehow the old man succeeded in freeing one hand – the other, according to some accounts (and here, again, we must be wary of the ghoulish sensationalism for which broadside accounts were notorious) still bound to the stool on which he sat, and snatched at the noose, preventing the rope from tightening – and condemning himself to the same slow strangulation suffered by the young house-breaker. Then, according to William Drysdale (this time, thankfully, relying on his own recollection rather than second-hand storytelling), 'the hangman drew away the man's hand, pulled his legs, and amidst a guttural sound from his lips, and a yell from the excited crowd, [his] head fell to the side and he was dead'.

His corpse remained unclaimed. Neither Agnes – his daughter from his first marriage, and his only kin – nor the local kirk would take custody of his remains. Hastily dumped into a cheap pine box, he was buried beneath the new step then being laid by the pend leading from the ground-floor cells into Jail Wynd. Here he remained – his spectre routinely blamed for all manner of minor mishaps within the Tolbooth during subsequent decades – until his grave was uncovered during renovations by conservation architects Simpson and Brown, in 2000. Other remains were also discovered at this time, including those believed to belong to 'Scatters' – Alexander Millar – a local thug whose principal claim to fame, as related in Geoff Holder's *The Guide To Mysterious Stirlingshire* (2008), was a futile attempt to cheat death, according to a prophesy that he would *die with his boots on*, by kicking his shoes into the crowd from the gallows, on 8 April 1837.

4

'AGAINST GOD AND THE KING'

Witchcraft

No account of crime and punishment in the Royal Burgh would be complete without at least a brief look at local prosecutions for witchcraft, the greatest concentration of such cases in Scotland occurring between 1590 and 1680. A crime against both the laws of God and State, it had the almost unique distinction of being tried by representatives of *both*, in turn.

In the first instance accusations of witchcraft were brought to the attention of the Minister and the Kirk Session, who, under the authority of the Presbytery, would examine witnesses to establish whether the accused was guilty of malefic (malicious) intent, or of the lesser charge of *charming*. If there was deemed to be sufficient grounds to proceed, the accused would be detained, tortured to secure a confession – or, rather, to prove the *veracity* of any confession offered; only then was an accusation deemed to be *proven*, and the secular authorities – the Burgh or Sheriff Court, or, in a small number of cases, Edinburgh's Privy Court – engaged in conducting a formal trial. Conviction for witchcraft in Scotland generally resulted in hanging (or strangulation) and burning at the stake.

In most cases, mercifully, the treatment of witches in the Burgh was comparatively bloodless. The thumbikins (thumbscrews) are known to have been used in the extraction of confession, here, but despite easy access to the waters of the River Forth there is no record of a Ducking Stool being used in Stirling, nor of the use of more grotesque tools of persuasion favoured in Scots witch-trials, which included:

- The pilniewinks, a finger vice which gradually crushed each digit from fingertip to knuckle
- The boot, which performed the same service to the bones of the foot
- The cashielaws, an iron cage fitted around the legs of the accused, allowing them to be raised, turned and toasted over a burning brazier

Down to the valley: landscaped in the 1850s as part of a Victorian extension to the Holy Rude cemetery, the valley was host to the weekly Horse Market, and to occasional witch burning - at a safe distance from the thatched roofs of the town. (Photo by Patricia Brannigan)

The cashielaws was a favourite of King James VII, who officiated at many such trials, and whose book, *On Daemonologie* (1597) is a veritable guidebook for the would-be witch-finder, seeking spiritual and political justification for his state-sanctioned sadism. The cashielaws had been a gift from his father-in-law, Frederick II of Denmark, to mark the occasion of James's marriage to his daughter, Anne. James's fervour for witch-finding was infamous, as evidenced by his brutal treatment of the alleged North Berwick witches in 1590.

One Stirling woman may well have fallen victim to the King's unwholesome appetite. On 16 September 1597 James wrote to the Provost and Bailies of Stirling, demanding that they immediately despatch a 'prickat witch', then being held in the Tolbooth, for trial at his palace in Linlithgow. The fate of this unfortunate creature is not recorded. Nor, indeed, is her name or any other details of her alleged crimes (the Burgh's evident distaste for this brutal business is manifest, chiefly, in poor record-keeping where such crimes are concerned), other than that, having been 'prickat' – her flesh pierced with a bodkin, a long thin blade – she had already endured the initial stages of examination. It was common belief that the Devil, on taking the soul of a living being, marked their flesh. If located, these 'Devil's Marks' – usually moles, birthmarks and naturally occurring blemishes – would be pierced. If no blood issued forth, their guilt was assured and their *unnatural* status confirmed. Of course the lack of blood was *entirely* natural: the bodkin having been heated in a brazier prior to pricking, the wound would be immediately cauterized – which may go some way to explaining the exceptionally high rate of convictions amongst those accused witches who had reached this stage of examination. Witch-finders in Scotland, sanctioned under the King's authority, were known as 'common prickers'. The accused's oft-reported imperviousness to pain on being pricked can be easily put down to shock, exacerbated by the sleep-deprivation: 'waking the witch' being another traditional means employed by interrogators intent on gaining a confession by inducing hallucination.

'Alle excuses sett aparte'

Comparatively, few Stirling witches endured examination at the hands of professional 'prickers', and James himself may have believed the Bailies and Burgesses of the Burgh dangerously soft-hearted in their consideration of those charged with dabbling in the dark arts. In demanding that the 'prickat witch' be brought before him, he warned that they should 'fail not (alle excuses sett aparte)'. If so, then he was not without some justification.

In the earliest recorded prosecution, from September 1562, Jonet Lyndesay and her daughter Isabel Keir were simply drummed out of town; 'an na man to persew thame theirfoir'. They were lucky to escape with their lives: the following year, the Reformed Kirk was to instigate the *Witchcraft Act* (1563), making theirs – according to the Mosaic Law, recorded in *Exodus* 22:18 ('Thou shalt not suffer a witch to live') – a capital offence. Even under instruction of the local Kirk Session, who bid in July 1612 that all parishioners remain vigilant of Satan and all His works, and 'tak inquisition quair any sic thing is committed and as they find to tak ordur yarwaith as appertainis and to discharge ye samin publictlie in pulpet', there seems to be considerable evidence of such sufferance in Stirling.

Questioned about the alleged charming of her neighbours in 1613, healer and herbalist Isobell Atkine of Jushie freely confessed to the charge, but stubbornly refused to cease-and-desist her ministrations. The frustrated Presbytery eventually upgraded her charge to witchcraft, but, there being no proof of *malefic* intent, opted only to excommunicate her, on 16 August 1615 – two years *after* she had first been investigated by the Kirk Session. Jonet Tailzour, the fabled 'Witch of Monza', was brought before the Presbytery, in 1633. Jonet had, until recently, enjoyed some considerable reputation as a healer. She had famously 'unwitched' the sickly Barbara

Dawson by washing her in south-running water, cutting her hair and nails and baking them in a bannock, which was then burned in order that what ailed her might pose no threat to others. For unspecified reasons – most likely a spate of cures unsurprisingly resistant to the placebo effect offered by her favoured form of sympathetic magic – public sentiment had turned against Tailzour and she was condemned, along with three other notorious (if slightly less celebrated) wise-women, Helen Keir and Jonet and Marion Mathie, of cursing those she had been charged to cure. According to the minutes of the Kirk Session, she was ordered to be drummed out of the town and banished 'in alle time', a fine of £10 to be levied on anyone who offered her aid or shelter (confusingly, Presbytery records for the same period state that she was burned at the stake). The following year, Elizabeth Spittal and Agnes Christie were tried for the rather more bloody act of killing a bitch in heat, and cutting out its liver for use in a love potion. Carted through the town and banished, they too were spared the full weight of *Moses' Law*.

Tacit toleration of practitioners of traditional cures rarely extended to those whose rituals were of recent origin. The vague charge of Witchcraft brought against Denny woman Margaret Crawford, in the early months of 1596, seem to originate in suspicions that she observed Roman Catholic Communion rites (prohibited in staunchly Protestant Scotland since 1560). Turning a blind eye to traditional healers was one thing for the Presbytery, toleration of what R.S. Fleming was still, in 1898, deriding as 'Popery and its attendant superstitions', was quite another.

Incidentally, the very act of seeking the aid of a suspected witch could lead to prosecution or punishment. In January 1628, Helen Squyar and Margaret Donaldsoune were brought before the Session. On Margaret's behest, Helen had taken a shirt belonging to her friend's child to be charmed by a carlin-wife at Garlickcraig. For the encouragement of such God-less immorality, the pair were made to make a public act of contrition, seated upon the Penance Stool before the congregation. Similar penance was demanded of Burgess John Gibsone and Agnes Hamiltoune, in 1677, when they sought the aid of supposed local seer, 'the dumb man Christie', in locating the whereabouts of a quantity of stolen cloth.

In September 1658, Kathrin Black was arrested, tried and convicted as a witch. Detained within the Tolbooth she had been released briefly, in December, on the order of the Privy Council, the conditions of her confinement having blighted her with the 'bloody flux' – dysentery. By March 1659 she was again in good health, back in custody and awaiting transportation to the Americas, along with two other 'witches', Elizabeth Black and Elspeth Crockett. They were still waiting two years later when, in January 1661, the court ordered their retrial, due to unspecified irregularities in their original prosecutions. No record remains of the subsequent verdict. It is entirely possible that charges were dismissed. In 1677 three more witches and a warlock (a rarity for Stirling) were also transported.

The Blair Witch Project: the shrewd scheming of accused witch Magdalin Blair (portrayed in the 2010 Stirling GhostWalk by actress Patricia Brannigan) saved her from execution, but cost others dearly. (Photo by Patricia Brannigan)

In July 1590, Marion McNab of Knockhill was accused of spoiling malt through witchcraft and using charms upon the ailing husband of neighbour Jonet Mitchell. McNab denied the accusation, but did concede that she had – with Jonet – travelled to Kilmahog to consult a woman named McGilers who claimed that she could repair the malt. Detained in the custody of the Laird of Logie, she faced twenty-two witnesses brought by Mitchell to testify as to her malice. A seemingly endless parade of local worthies called by both women proceeded before the Session on 11, 18 and 25 August, and the accusation against McNab was finally deemed to have been *proven* on 15 September. Released, she was ordered to present herself before the Sheriff when called to face a civil trial. No further reference is made to her in records, and, again, the dismissal of charges against her is not unlikely.

It is to the credit of the local population – and, if truth be told, to the otherwise reactionary Kirk Session – that it was largely resistant to the witch-hunting hysteria which blighted Britain in the sixteenth and seventeenth centuries, and that so few of the accusations of witchcraft brought before them were taken further than preliminary public examination. It was common, too, for counter-suit for slander to be brought by the accused. In 1587, Marjorie Robertsoune had been accused by her neighbour, Margaret Ritchie, of using magic to take milk from her father's cow. Witnesses having been called and testimony given, the Presbytery judged that Margaret was guilty of malicious slander, and she was made publicly to beg the forgiveness of God, the congregation and Maistress Robertsone, herself. On 4 September 1690, Jonet Mitchell accused Robert Kerr and his wife of calling her a witch in public, and claiming that she had used charms to harm the health of their child. Their slander proven to the satisfaction of the Session, the Kerrs were thrown into the Tolbooth, pending payment of a hefty £50 fine. In 1698 Helen Duncanson brought suit against her daughter-in-law, Elizabeth Paterson, on similar grounds (though this pair were simply exhorted to settle their differences and 'live Christianly together'). Even in cases when the Session felt a case was *proven*, the civil authorities were often reluctant to act. From 1697 until 1699 the Presbytery were insistent that a group of women from Larbert who had been 'turning the riddle' – fortune telling – be prosecuted by the Provost and Bailies. They declined, and the women were subject to no more than the scorn and censure of the kirk.

The Blair Witch

In isolation, as the previous examples have shown, the traditional view that there was no legal counter-argument to a charge of witchcraft simply does *not* hold true. In cases of individual accusation it was entirely possible to escape death or defer physical punishment. This was not, sadly, always the case, even in Stirling.

In January 1659, Magdalin Blair was denounced by her neighbour Helen Ker, who claimed that she had brought about the death of another neighbour's horse through charms. Having confronted Magdalin, Ker had returned home to discover a grotesque lump of flesh in the shape of a hand between the sheets of her bed. Soon afterwards, she became ill. Accusations against Blair did not stop there. The physical and financial woes of local burgess John Steill, who had 'gotten a bairn with her and would give her nothing' for its upkeep, were also attributed to Magdalin's malice. Helen Ferguson swore that she had been cursed for an unspecified 'unkindnesse' to the witch's husband. Blair, in turn, accused Helen of seeking the services of another 'consulting charmer', Katherine Greg. William Luckison, maltman, testified that Magdalin had offered to cure him of a sickness placed upon him by Isobel Bennet (a friend, it can be no coincidence, of Helen Ferguson). Isobel was then tried alongside the accused. Blair then implicated another healer, Bessie Stivenson. Bessie gave account of fashioning charms from fragments of a horseshoe shed by a beast borne by fairies, of anointing cripples with waters borne 'from the hollows of the sea', and of curing those who were 'maw-turned' (afflicted by nausea) by leading them in a merry dance around an oak tree while repeating a charm. Her testimony provides a fascinating, colourful and genuinely *charming* account of the folk magic of the era – which may have been why she was named by the shrewd Maistress Blair. As Geoff Holder – whose *The Guide to Mysterious Stirlingshire* offers a more comprehensive guide to witchcraft cases in the area than is possible here – notes, 'cleverly, Magdalin…seems to have implicated two people with rather more "form" than herself.' The case against her *unproven* – relying only on the testimony of those known to have grudges against her – she walked free. The others were not so fortunate. Brought before the Burgh Court, Isobel Bennet was convicted of *charming*, whipped through the streets and fined £20. Poor harmless Bessie was burned at the stake on 1 April 1659, the judgement against her rendered all the more remarkable by the complete lack of *malice* evident in her testimony. It did, however, occur in the wake of a genuinely shocking spate of accusations and executions, the previous year, in which – as with most such panics – talk of 'pacts with the devil' featured prominently.

On 23 June 1658, accused witch Margaret Duchil from Alloa is said to have surprised her interrogators with sudden claims that she had been in the service of Satan for twenty years, having first made his acquaintance 'in the likeness of a man in brown clothes and a black hat' who seduced her at the home of Logie woman, Isobel Jameson. He 'caused me to lie on my face and had to do with me and grunkled over me like a sow', she said. Later he asked, 'Maggie, will ye be my servant?' and, when she agreed, put his Devil's Mark upon her. Margaret went on to describe two decades of cattle affliction, shape-shifting, assault and the murder of (amongst others) Bessie Vertie, Jonet Houston and the infant daughter of burgess John Demperstone. Asked by the Court 'what women should be burned if she were burned', she immediately named neighbours Elspeth and Jonet Black, Bessie Paton, Margaret Tailor and Katherine (or Bessie) Rainie, all of whom had variously danced with the Devil and flown through the air in her presence, atop the hilltop now known as the Witches' Crag. Geoff Holder reports a suggestion by P.G. Maxwell-Stuart, in *An Abundance of Witches* (2005) that these claims were so far removed from those contained in most contemporary confessions of Scottish witchcraft (those of Auldearn's Isobel Gowdie, in 1662 and *Steine Maltman* in 1628, may be of particular interest to folklorists seeking rather more representative accounts) that they may simply have been taken from some contemporary account of diabolism – Martin Del Rio's *Disquisitiones Magicae* (1624) is suggested – and inserted into Duchil's narrative by ambitious interrogators eager to make a name for themselves. The possibilities that Duchil, broken by torture and near to death, had simply agreed to *any* charges suggested to her by her tormentors, or that she was maliciously striking out at those she bore a grudge against, cannot be discounted. However fantastic her claims may seem to us, they were seriously considered by

Witch hunt: the 'Witches' Crag', viewed from the Logie Kirk. Did those accused by Margaret Duchil really meet here, or was her confession the result of trial and torture? (Photo by David Kinnaird)

the court. Satan, in the eyes of the Presbytery, was a clear and present danger to the person, the parish and the state. Whether their ends were the result of greed, deception, delusion or simple old-fashioned spite, all of those accused by Margaret Duchil were convicted of witchcraft in Alloa on 3 August 1658, and burned at the stake in Edinburgh one week later. Other such panics occurred in smaller, rural tributaries to the town (in Larbert, Alloa, and Tullibody, for example) but they were mercifully rare.

The costs to the Burgh of burning a condemned witch may also go a little further in explaining why such executions were unpopular amongst Stirling's parsimonious protectors of law and order. Fleming's *Old Nooks of Stirling* details the cost of one such immolation, from 1652, conducted in the 'valley' – then site of the weekly Horse Market, and now part of the prettily landscaped 1854 extension to the Holy Rude cemetery:

Items, spent with Johne Mellines and other wrychts and the officeris quhen they were aggreit with to mak up the gallowes in the valley – £1 6s 0d

Item, for two spars to be the gallowes and for two dailies and two tar barrellis – £3 17s 4d

Item, for peatts and colles to the execution – £5 9s 0d

Item, to the officiris eftir the execution – £0 12s 0d

Item, to the hangman quhen he went away – £8 0s 0d

Payit to John Eglintoun for garnishing meat and drink to the thieves and witches that cam frae Perth to the justice air – £4 0s 0d

The last execution for witchcraft in Scotland would not occur until 1727, more than forty years after the final prosecution in Stirling, that of Elizabeth Naesmith, in 1683. As with the vast majority of cases brought before the Session during those decades of ever increasing scepticism and disdain for superstition, it was 'deserted without charge'.

Traitors to the Crown

It is possibly surprising, given Stirling's status as a seat of kings, and as the strategic 'Key to the Kingdom' – militarily dividing north from south and Highland from Lowland – that more cases of High Treason against the Crown and its interests are not recorded here. Though not executed in Stirling, part of the remains of William Wallace (d.1305) were displayed here by the English overlords – Stirling being the location of his famous victory

Hanged, drawn and quartered: the National Wallace Monument celebrates William's victory over the English at Stirling Bridge. As punishment for his 'Treason' against the invader he was publicly butchered, parts of his corpse displayed in Stirling to deter other would-be rebels. (Photo by David Kinnaird)

Covenanting cleric: a statue of James
Guthrie watches over the Holy
Rude kirk, divided - literally and
metaphorically - by political strife in
his lifetime. (Photo by David Kinnaird)

over the English army, in 1297 – as a warning to other rebellious Scots intent on opposing
King Edward I's occupation. Tried for High Treason at Westminster Hall, Wallace refused
to acknowledge the authority of the court. Having never sworn allegiance to the English
Crown – unlike many Scots nobles who signed an oath of fealty, known disparagingly as
the 'Ragmans' Roll', (amongst them Robert Bruce, soon to become King Robert I) – he
could hardly be condemned for *disloyalty* to it. Stripped naked and dragged to the Elms at
Smithfield, he was partially strangled upon a gib, revived, castrated, eviscerated – his bowels
being burned before him – then beheaded. His corpse cut into four parts, his limbs were
displayed in Newcastle, Berwick-upon-Tweed, Aberdeen and, of course, Stirling.

We have already touched upon the circumstances of the unfortunate end of James
I's rivals, the Albany Stewarts, on Mote Hill (see Chapter 1), but a small number of
cases of dissent are worthy of attention.

A Dissenting Cleric

One minor pre-Reformation *heretic* was said to have been burned by the Roman
Catholic authorities, and, following John Knox's first visit to the Holy Rude

– 'purged of idolatry' on his instruction, it's idols and statues smashed by the townsfolk – two priests were sentenced to death. Mercifully, their sentence was remitted: stripped of their vestments they were pelted with 'nastiness', and banished. Although it relates to a punishment which did not itself occur in Stirling, the story of Mr James Guthrie, Minister of the Church if the Holy Rude between 1649 and 1661, is perhaps the most significant instance of religious dissent within the town in the seventeenth century – and one directly related to numerous subsequent prosecutions and penalties within the area.

A Protestant fundamentalist, Guthrie had, while Minister to the kirk at Lauder, railed against Charles I's attempts in the 1630s to introduce an Episcopalian liturgy into the Church of Scotland, an affront in the eyes of many, to the terms of the 1560 *Confession of Faith* – long since adopted by the General Assembly of the kirk – which formally denounced such *Papist* notions as government by bishops. This first faltering step toward intended unity between the Anglican and native Presbyterian kirks, had been initiated by James VI in 1584. While he supported Scots radicals in their ardent efforts against Charles' ecclesiastical ambitions, in what became known as the Bishops Wars (or *Bellum Episcopale*) of 1639-40, he remained convinced of the King's (literally) *God-given* right to rule, describing Lord Protector Oliver Cromwell, following Charles' execution and the establishment of the Commonwealth as 'ane usurper'. Stirling was as divided as the radicals, who has agreed a 'Solemn League and Covenant' with the English Parliamentarians in 1643 (on the understanding that the Scots form of church government be adopted in England, and entered into an 'Engagement' with Charles against Parliamentary dissenters, the English Independents, five years later (the King having agreed that Presbyterianism should be adopted by the Anglican clergy for three years). Early Royalist defeat in this campaign rendered the agreement void, and forever soured relations with the Commonwealth. Largely monarchist by inclination – Stirling was, after all, a *Royal Burgh* – it was with great reluctance that the magistrates ordered that the citizenry yield to General Monck's army after a brief and bloody siege of the castle, on 6 August 1561. The Bailies and officers were obliged to swear an oath of loyalty to Cromwell's government:

> You shall swear that you shall be true and faithful to the Commonwealth of England as it is now established without a King or House of Lords; you shall well and truly execute [your office] within the town and burgh of Stirling and the liberties thereof according to the best of your skill, knowledge and power. So help you God.

The Earl of Mar was suspended from his duties as keeper of the castle, and English troops began a lengthy occupation of the fortress. Many local Burgesses were sympathetic to the Royalist cause, and even welcomed the ideal of Episcopalian

The star pyramid: built by William Drummond to a design by William Barclay in 1863, the pyramid, known as 'Salem's Rock', is a memorial to those who died in consequence of their opposition to the Episcopacy. (Photo by David Kinnaird)

Castle Wynd – The unfortunate ninth Earl of Argyll paid the price for his father's disloyalty to the Crown. (Image reproduced by kind permission of the Stirling Smith Art Gallery and Museum)

Church Government. Others, including the majority of the townsfolk, local craftsmen, and James Guthrie – who by this time had been Minister of the Holy Rude for twelve years – were rendered even more defiantly protective of the presbytery by English occupation. As the Burgh was divided, so – quite literally – was the church, one irate entry in the records complaining that the Holy Rude itself had been separated into two churches by a partition wall erected by 'James Guthrie, sometime a minister of this congregation (but now deposed by the church) and a few persons of the incorporations (whereof some pretend to be elders)'. William Drysdale, in *Auld Biggins of Stirling: Its Closes, Wynds and Neebour Villiages* (1904) reports a local tradition that members of certain trades took violent exception to Guthrie's refusal to adopt the Episcopalian liturgy 'and almost stoned to death' by members of the Incorporation of Fleshers, reporting that 'a stone for some time was shown in the Vennel Close upon which some of his blood was said to have been spilt.' For their impudence, the great storyteller tells us, 'no flesher ever did good' in the town – prompting the lines by Ralph Erskine:

> O, Stirling, Stirling, thou hast been the seat
> Of famous martyrs and confessors great;
> Some thou hast stoned by the fierce butcherous hive,
> Which never since has had a day to thrive.

The tale alluded to actually predates Guthrie by more than a century, the butchers' curse supposedly bestowed by an early Protestant martyr, robbed and beaten by a local butcher's wife, unsympathetic to his reforming views. Either way, Stirling was a place divided.

The 'deposed' Minister and his flock continued to congregate for many years, the partition remaining in place until the 1930s. Guthrie was arrested for Treason, following Charles II's Restoration, in 1660. After a short trial within the castle's Great Hall, he was hanged in Edinburgh on 1 June 1661, his head displayed upon the Netherbow Port for a further twenty-seven years. His statue is amongst those which decorate the Victorian kirkyard. *The Sedition Act* (1661) declared the 'Solemn League and Covenant' unlawful and in Stirling, as elsewhere, was ordered to be burned at the Mercat Cross 'by the hands of the common hangman'. In the years that followed, many Covenanting sympathisers, Guthrie supporters amongst them, found themselves arrested for apostasy or attending conventicles, or simply victimised by Stirling Bailies eager to iterate their loyalty to the new Episcopalian monarch. Craftsman Alexander Burne and his wife, for example, spent several months in the Tolbooth on the ludicrous charge of cohabiting unlawfully (their ceremony having been performed by the 'deposed' Guthrie). Such treatment occurred with the approval of the Privy Council.

Following the fall of Charles' successor, the Catholic James VIIII, and the 1689 re-establishment of a staunchly Protestant co-regency under William II and Mary II, the ecclesiastical shoe was once more on the other foot, as Guthrieites regained control of Stirling's Council. Episcopalian cleric Adam Peacock found himself briefly imprisoned in the Tolbooth in January 1703, as was Doune schoolmaster James Wingate, held there four years earlier, who refused to recognise the authority of the Kirk Session 'since the ministers were not ordained by a Bishop nor the judicature constituted in his name'. After a few short days in the cells he was released – having offered a contrite confession that he 'was troubled that he should have been so rash' and 'promised all submission' to the Session.

In the shadow of Stirling Castle stands the finest surviving example of a seventeenth-century Scottish townhouse, Argyll's Ludging, home, from the early 1670s, of Archibald Campbell, ninth Earl of Argyll – often styled as another martyr for the Covenanting cause. Archibald had inherited the Earldom in 1663, two years after his proudly Presbyterian father's execution for Treason by Charles II. A rather more cautious and considered statesman than that impetuous Covenanter, Archibald was to inherit, by association, the taint of disloyalty. Eager to display his loyalty to Charles, but equally committed to his father's faith, the ninth Earl was profoundly troubled by the imposition of the *Test Bill* (1681), which obliged it's aristocratic signatories to conform to whatever religion the King should himself choose. As Charles' most likely heir was his Catholic brother James, it was with great reluctance that Argyll accepted the oath, describing it diplomatically as 'consistent with itself'. In hesitating he left himself vulnerable to the slanders of his rivals, who saw his reluctance as proof that he was as inconstant and treacherous as his sire. To defend his title the imprisoned Earl staged a daring escape and, in 1685, swept away on a tide of events he could not fully control, led a catastrophic Highland rebellion against the newly crowned James. A most reluctant martyr, he was beheaded in Edinburgh's infamous 'Maiden' (currently displayed in the National Museum of Scotland) on Monday, 30 June 1685.

The Union Martyrs

Historically speaking, Stirling lacked both the industrial militancy of Glasgow and the civic volatility of Edinburgh. It was, however, to be host to the last public executions for Treason on Scottish soil, those of weavers John Baird and Andrew Hardie.

Following the end of the Napoleonic Wars, in 1815, Britain was in crisis. Unemployment was soaring, many labourers having been left jobless as long established communities were decimated by the sweeping changes effected by rapid industrial and rural mechanisation. The Corn Laws, introduced that same year, protected the profits

A bloody end: the executioner's cloak and axe used during the beheading of Baird and Hardie in 1822. (Photo reproduced by kind permission of the Stirling Smith Art Gallery & Museum)

and political power of landowners by stemming the flow of cheap imported grain, but left much of the population hungry. In the south, attempts to organise trade unions, defending the rights of workers were violently crushed by the Tory government of Robert Banks Jenkinson, Lord Liverpool, and public meetings by prominent agitators and pamphleteer such as William Cobbett, advocating parliamentary reform and the institution of voting rights for ordinary citizens – only 2 per cent of the population then enjoying that particular privilege – were brutally broken up by armed troops.

Inevitably this urban radicalism moved northward. In April 1820 posters appeared in Scotland's cities, urging the common people to support a national strike and the formation of a new revolutionary government. A week of protests, led largely by militant weavers and other artisans – henceforth dubbed the 'Radical War' – ensued. In Glasgow, where such militancy was not unknown and some form of insurrection was expected, preparations were made to pre-empt trouble. Barricades were erected around public buildings, and on Monday 3 April cavalry were despatched to disperse the thousands of demonstrators gathering in the city centre. Similar scenes of post-war militancy were witnessed in that same place a century later, during the Battle of George Square on Bloody Friday – 19 January 1919 – when Minister of Munitions, Winston Churchill (insistent that militancy should be 'strangled in its cradle'), authorised the deployment of tanks and troops, armed with machine guns and howitzers on the city streets. Stirling and its environs *would* see some disruption during the later General Strike of 1926, but its workers – then, as in 1820 – were not considered to pose a significant threat.

As the 1822 Glasgow protests commenced, weaver John Craig led a group of thirty men in a march to the Carron Company ironworks, hoping to seize arms and munitions held there. Intercepted by Hussars waiting in ambush for radicals fleeing the troops deployed in Glasgow, Craig was captured and fined (the fine, surprisingly, paid for him by a Bailie sympathetic to his cause). The following day the mantle of leadership was passed to Andrew Hardie, who led around sixty men, some of them already armed, on a slow march to Carron. Struggling through driving wind and rain, his group was reduced to a weary and bedraggled twenty-five by the time

For justice and truth: a memorial to Baird and Hardie was mounted on Gideon Grey's extension to the Tolbooth townhouse by the local Labour Party in 1966. (Photo by David Kinnaird)

it reached Condorrat, where they were joined by John Baird. Hopeful that they would find more support from like-minded workers at Camelon, the group left the main road and made for Bonnymuir. The Hussars, having scattered Craig's group, had been instructed to return to the ironworks and stand guard. Alerted to the intentions of Hardie's men they made straight for Bonnymuir where, on seeing them, as reported in the following day's *Glasgow Herald*, 'the radicals cheered and advanced to a wall over which they commenced firing at the military. Some shots were then fired by the soldiers'. After some time the soldiers succeeded in 'taking nineteen of them prisoner, who are lodged in Stirling Castle'. John Baird and Andrew Hardie were amongst them. '[The] Conspiracy appears more extensive than almost anyone imagined' complained the *Herald*, fearful as to the extent of popular support enjoyed by the would-be insurrectionists; 'radical principles are too widely spread and too deeply rooted to vanish without some explosion, and the sooner it takes place the better.'

An example was necessary to stifle what the *Stirling Journal* termed a 'shameful militancy'. All in all forty-seven radicals were detained, including many who had departed the procession long before the conflict at Bonnymuir. Of these, three were to be tried for High Treason, and most others transported. James Wilson, judged guilty by the court of 'compassing to levy war against the King in order to compel him to change his measures', was hanged and beheaded at Glasgow, and the trial of Baird and Hardie – accused of, amongst other things, 'imagining the death of the King' – commenced on 13 July at Stirling's Tolbooth. The conclusion was inevitable. 'I can hold out little or no hope of mercy', advised the Judge: an example was necessary, and 'as you were the leaders, I am afraid that example must be given by you.'

Their case, and the events of their execution, on 8 September 1820, were to enjoy much greater national coverage in the newspapers than would normally be the case for the proceedings of a provincial court. Strict censorship and the obvious political bias of many publishers renders somewhat suspect the veracity of many contemporary accounts – there is a great disparity between the sensationalist sentimentality of the broadsides, the dogged *party-line* taken in C. J. Green's *Trials for High Treason in Scotland* (1825) in its thuggish depiction of the radicals, and the rather more cautious and considered observations of the regional press – but the basic facts do not appear to be in doubt. Dundee's *Courier* wrote that:

> This day at one o'clock, the Sheriff's Depute and Substitute of the County of Stirling, accompanied by the Magistrates, and proceeded by the Town and Sheriff's Officers, went in procession from the Town-house to the Castle, to receive the prisoners at the Castle gate. They were met by the Lieutenant-Governor, General Graham, when the Sheriff demanded the two prisoners, Hardie and Baird. The gates were thrown open and a strong party of the 13th [Regiment of Foot]…marched out and formed two lines, one on each side of the road. A squadron of the 7th Dragoon Guards were already drawn up outside the Castle gate, and when the prisoners arrived, formed outside the infantry, and also in front and rear of the procession. The prisoners, who were decently dressed in black clothes, with weepers and crepe, attended by the three Ministers of the Established Church, now came out of the Castle, and mounted the hurdle with a firm and undaunted mien.

If the demeanour of the condemned men mounting the cart to greet the black-hooded executioner was calmly 'firm and undaunted', his axe resting on his thigh, the same could *not* be said of the authorities. For every four inhabitants of the town, there was one armed soldier present. The Glasgow hangman engaged to despatch the pair had been secretly escorted into the town two days before, fearful for his safety, and remained hooded throughout proceedings. The calmness with which the weavers sat in prayer within the Tolbooth was unsettling. The *Courier* continued:

The executioner was then called in to pinion the prisoners. This they submitted to, almost cheerfully…declaring that they were now ready to proceed to the scaffold.

The gallows had been prepared 'with all the insignia of death', and a coffin positioned on each side. To the left lay the wooden block for decapitation. The Sheriff, Ranald MacDonald – Bonnymuir falling within the rural rubric of his authority – had demanded that the pair make no political speech from the scaffold, but agreed that they could speak upon Scripture. Baird began in the required tone of the Broadside penitents, *The Times* of London reporting his heartfelt musings the crowd. 'I entreat you, notice your Bibles, and conduct yourself soberly; mind religion at all times; but be not regardless of Justice and Reason on every subject.' He then added, with rather more venom, 'Although this day we die an ignominious death by unjust laws, our blood, which in a very few minutes will flow over this scaffold, will cry to Heaven for vengeance, and may it be the means of our afflicted Countrymen's speedy redemption.' Concerned that further passionate proclamations might provoke the crowd to violence – though as *The Times* noted, it was to 'the credit of the humanity of the inhabitants of this place, very few attended the execution…[and] the crowd seemed almost entirely composed of people from the country, this being the market-day' – Hardie was discouraged from further agitations. Instead he bid the crowd, as the *Courier* observed, 'not go to public houses to drink to the memory of Baird and Hardie, but go home and think of God, and mend their lives', though he, too, could not resist one last defiant cry: 'I die a martyr to the cause of truth and justice.' A cheer from the crowd followed, then a brief, panicked retreat into the surrounding closes and alleys as the anxious troops, still half-expecting riot and rampage, raised their weapons. There was no need: order was restored, and the executions continued without interruption.

The pair knelt, and the black hooded cap and noose was put over the head of each man in turn. They held hands, prayed for a moment, and Baird sang the first verse of the fifth Psalm:

Give ear unto my words, O Lord, my meditations weigh.
Hear my loud cry, my King, my God; for I to thee will pray.
Lord, thou shalt early hear my voice: I early will direct
My pray'r to thee; and, looking up, an answer will expect.

This manages, in its way, to be a far more militant call-to-action than his previous outburst. On a signal from Hardie, the *Courier* continues, 'they were immediately thrown off and died without a struggle. Baird kept his copy of the New Testament in his hand, and it afterwards fell on the street.' After hanging for half an hour, the pair were cut down, and preparations for the final requirement of the

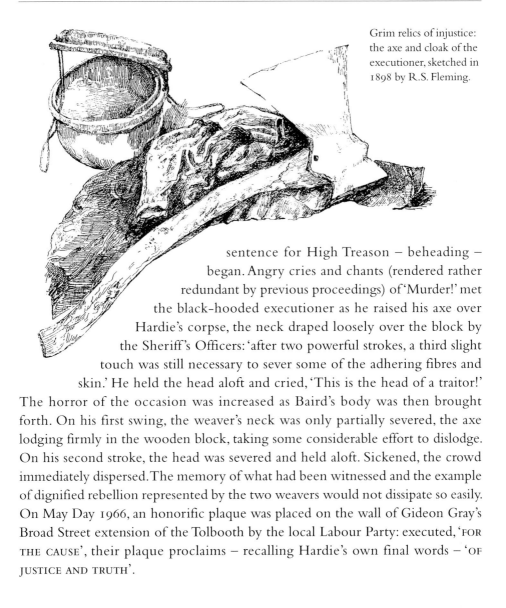

Grim relics of injustice:
the axe and cloak of the
executioner, sketched in
1898 by R.S. Fleming.

sentence for High Treason – beheading –
began. Angry cries and chants (rendered rather
redundant by previous proceedings) of 'Murder!' met
the black-hooded executioner as he raised his axe over
Hardie's corpse, the neck draped loosely over the block by
the Sheriff's Officers: 'after two powerful strokes, a third slight
touch was still necessary to sever some of the adhering fibres and
skin.' He held the head aloft and cried, 'This is the head of a traitor!'
The horror of the occasion was increased as Baird's body was then brought
forth. On his first swing, the weaver's neck was only partially severed, the axe
lodging firmly in the wooden block, taking some considerable effort to dislodge.
On his second stroke, the head was severed and held aloft. Sickened, the crowd
immediately dispersed. The memory of what had been witnessed and the example
of dignified rebellion represented by the two weavers would not dissipate so easily.
On May Day 1966, an honorific plaque was placed on the wall of Gideon Gray's
Broad Street extension of the Tolbooth by the local Labour Party: executed, 'FOR
THE CAUSE', their plaque proclaims – recalling Hardie's own final words – 'OF
JUSTICE AND TRUTH'.

5

A NEW COUNTY JAIL

A Place of Penance

In the 1760s and 1770s, Hackney-born philanthropist John Howard had made an extensive study of many prisons throughout Great Britain, collecting his findings in a horrific catalogue of abuse, neglect and mismanagement, *The State of Prisons in England and Wales* (1777). Here, his proposals for the radical redress of the 'problem of crime' were clearly laid down. Prisoners, first and foremost, should be separated according to their sex and the extent of their criminality; solitude was necessary to encourage reflection and repentance; the physical wellbeing of inmates should not be neglected, and adequate dietary provision, accommodation and exercise provided; religious observance should be mandatory; finally, jailors should be properly paid, thus preventing them from selling alcohol or accepting bribes from felons in order to supplement their incomes. Readers will have already noted that Stirling's Tolbooth, known to have been visited by Howard, though his opinions of that place are not recorded in his most famous work, fails on every count. Crime statistics were continuing to rise, prisons were full to capacity, and the Transportation of radicals and dissenters to the Americas had clearly been a factor in encouraging revolution within His Majesty's Colonies in 1776. It was clear that if the traditional means of controlling the criminal classes – the corporal punishment, court-sanctioned mutilation and banishments we have witnessed on previous pages – were insufficient to the task of maintaining an orderly society, more radical methods *must* be tried. Felons must be *reformed*, and for that to happen they must be properly *contained* and effectively *conditioned* to repent through the processes of standardized custodial sentences. Howard's ideas were to influence many other celebrated reformers, including Samuel Romily and Elizabeth Fry, and, through them, the likes of Frederick Hill.

In April 1841 – pre-empting the publication of Hill's *Summary Report* condemning the Tolbooth as the 'worst jail in Britain' by a matter of months – the County Prison Board recommended that the sum of £5,000 be provided for the purpose of

A new county jail: completed
in 1847 to replace the feared
and hated Tolbooth, it continues
to serve the town as a popular
visitor attraction – the Stirling
Old Town Jail. (Photo by David
Kinnaird)

Ordered symmetry: the cells
of the East Wing of the County
Jail, now offices, as viewed from
the Panopticon. (Photo by
David Kinnaird, courtesy
of Stirling District Tourism)

erecting a new County Jail. The project was to be funded jointly by the Stirling and Falkirk Town Councils and the Commissioners of Supply for the county. A further £1,200 was allocated for the purchase of a suitable site.

The Separate System

The new building was to be designed by Thomas Brown, appointed as architect to the Prison Board of Scotland in 1837, and would reflect the innovations of the Separate System gaining popularity through the work of Frederic Hill's friend and colleague, William Brebner. Brebner had encouraged the sustained separation of inmates as a tool of rehabilitation while serving as Governor of Glasgow's Bridewell Prison, and his approach to disciplined reform, which purposely encouraged self-reflection, would be developed by Hill in his influential *Crime: Its Amount, Causes and Remedies* (1853). No association was to be permitted, even between those convicts assigned to collective work duties in areas such as laundries or kitchens, where partitions (and the constant vigilance of Wardens and Matrons) would prevent any contact or conversation. Fifty-one cells, spread over five floors, and divided between two corridors extending outward from a central tower, would face a Panopticon – a vantage point from which the governor or chaplain could address the prison population without them leaving their cells (and without the need to construct a chapel or any other collective space) and each inmate could be kept under constant supervision. Walls, doors and in some cases floors were to be whitewashed in order to maximise available natural light, and a network of pipes and air-vents would effect the circulation of fresh air from two wells in the back courtyard. There was even to be a rudimentary central-heating system. Many aspects of Brown's design, including the Panopticon – 'the Gordian knot of the Poor Law not cut, but untied – all by a simple idea in Architecture' – are attributed to the innovative influence of political philosopher Jeremy Bentham in his book *Panopticon* (1785) – though Bentham, and, in turn, Brown and Brebner, actually owe a far more considerable debt to John Howard's proposals for an 'ideal penitentiary house' within the pages of *The State of Prisons*. The degradations offered by the binding folds of the Poor Law, so reviled by Bentham, were not entirely unravelled by this new prison movement: the new jail retained a Debtors' Day Room, where those in debt could be detained, at the expense of their creditors, until such time as monies owed might be settled by their friends, family or business associates. Unlike ordinary prisoners they, at least, were permitted to wear their own clothes and converse freely.

The local newspaper, the *Stirling Observer*, opposed the new endeavour from the start. What criminals needed was *punishment*, not *penitence*. Why should public funds

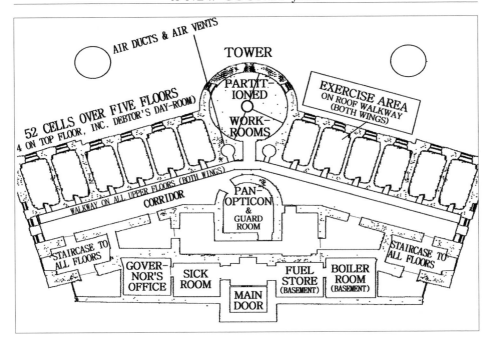

Supervision, security and solitude: The design of the new jail fulfilled the three main objectives of Brebner's 'Separate System'. (Illustration by David Kinnaird)

be profligately squandered on 'a parcel of rogues and vagabonds, and something worse than either'? The monies in question 'would erect comfortable habitations for one hundred families of respectable working men, who would willingly pay rent for them.' Many agreed, particularly as the ancient and overcrowded tenements of neighbouring Broad Street and St Mary's Wynd were quickly establishing themselves as the slums of Stirling. When, in 1844, provision for this ambitious endeavour proved insufficient and a further £4,000 was demanded to complete construction, the Councils staunchly refused to contribute further – only yielding when overcrowding in the Tolbooth required many prisoners to be sent to Perth and Edinburgh, and the Returns of the Keeper of that Jail, published in national newspapers, brought further scorn upon that institution and its administrators.

For many months those prisoners in the south-facing cells of the old jail would have seen and heard the slow, steady labour of workers constructing their new place of confinement. Finally, at 4 a.m. on the morning of 11 November 1847, they were marched from the overcrowded filthy huddle of the Tolbooth and entered the sparse, almost monastic environs of the new County Jail. Names were to be forgotten. In this brave new world a prisoner was to be known only by the number allocated to his cell. A final tally put the cost of completion at £9639 13s 4d (a little over half a million pounds in current currency).

New Rules and New Rights

The rules of the new institution were read over each new convict on their arrival – a process which could take more than an hour before the brow-beaten convict would be presented with his coarse grey uniform, tin cup and plate, and led to his cell. A selection from these regulations reveals a curious mix of restrictions intended to prevent persistent bad habits, encourage reflection, and ensure that physical and mental discipline was maintained at all times.

- If he be a criminal prisoner, his clothes and every other article in his possession shall be taken from him.
- An inventory shall be made of all articles taken or received from any prisoner, which shall be shown to the prisoner, and which, if he can write, he shall sign as evidence of his having examined it and found it correct.
- No prisoner's hair shall be cut against his will, except when necessary for health; it shall not be cut shorter than it is usually worn by people outside Prison. No prisoner's head shall be shaved.
- No prisoner shall be kept in a separate cell when the Surgeon is of opinion that it would be dangerous to his health or mind.
- It shall be shown to every prisoner that his cell and all the furnishings are clean and in good order, free from cutting, scribbling or other marks; and he shall be told that he will be required to keep it in that state.
- Except on Sunday, the time of rising for criminal prisoners shall not be later than six o'clock; and the period between rising and going to bed shall not be less than fifteen hours.
- Every criminal prisoner shall be required to do ten hours work each day, excluding Sundays.
- Every prisoner shall wash himself every morning and evening, Sunday inclusive, and he shall be required to wash his feet at least once a week.
- Male prisoners shall be shaved at least once a week.
- No profane or abusive language, and no quarrelling, or loud or disturbing noise of any kind shall be permitted.
- No card playing or game of chance of any kind, and no smoking, shall be allowed, and no Officer, or other person whatever, shall be permitted to smoke within the Prison grounds or buildings.

This was a radical departure from what went before. Strict, yes – and founded on a near-Spartan system of punitive self-discipline – but offering safeguards for the convicts themselves. Prisoners had *rights*, failure to observe which could have dire consequences for those charged to watch over them. Local tradition has it that the

REPORT ON SCOTTISH PRISONS.

FIFTEENTH REPORT OF THE INSPECTOR OF PRISONS FOR SCOTLAND.

STIRLING.

(Inspected May 9, 1849.)

Present in confinement:—

> 73 males.
> 26 females.
> ——
> Total......99

They made no complaints requiring notice.

The average daily number of prisoners in confinement for the past year has been 87, being one more than in 1848.

The governor complains that some of the upper cells take in rain at the windows, which ought to be remedied. The rain also beats in some places through the walls in stormy weather, which causes dampness in some of the cells.

I found the prison very clean, as were also the clothing and bedding, and the food of a good and wholesome quality.

There had been numerous cases of sickness, but no deaths; and the surgeon's duty seems to have been regularly and efficiently performed. He states, in his June Report, that during the prevalence of cholera he had found it necessary to double the allowance of animal food to the prisoners; but as the necessity has ceased to exist, he has intimated to the governor that the established dietary may be resumed.

A new chaplain, who also undertakes the duties of teacher, entered on his office on the 2d July last, and performs the same course of duty as his predecessor.

The governor remarks on the conduct of the prisoners, that, during their confinement, they have improved in temper and cleanliness, and, that a number of them have made a marked improvement in reading, writing, and arithmetic. Both he and the chaplain complain very much of the evil consequences of retaining convicts so long in such a prison as Stirling. There are 16 convicts here, 13 males and 3 females, 10 of them since September last. They were very troublesome and difficult to manage, the interior of the prison being defective in consequence of males and females occupying the same open galleries, and the means of communication through the cell windows, and from floor to floor, being so easy. I observed that one male prisoner had been punished for cutting his net to lower an ink-bottle to a female prisoner in the cell below him. The punishments have been numerous, but not of a serious character.

The chief employments are—

Weaving.	Teazing oakum.
Net-making.	Shoe-making.

The net cost per head has been £11 15s. 1d., and the average of the prison dietary £5 3s. 2d., which is a good deal lower than last year. The average amount of earnings, £2 16s. 3d.

The provisions and stores are all contracted for, except the bedding, clothing, oakum, and mattresses, which are bought at the cheapest market, and the accounts paid monthly to the contractors by the treasurer of the County Prison Board.

The governor settles his accounts quarterly with the treasurer, while the settlement is duly recorded in the cash-book.

The prison continues to be ably managed by Mr Campbell, the governor, and the subordinate officers seem zealous and efficient.

Early progress: within the new County Jail efforts were made to reform and rehabilitate prisoners, rather than simply punish them. (Author's collection) first Head Warder, a gruff Cumbrian ex-soldier named Hislop, horse-whipped one guard found pilfering prisoners' property. Many of those subjected to the solitary confinement of the original 'Separate System' experiments in numerous London prisons, having suffering long-lasting emotional distress, it was decreed that 'No prisoner shall be kept in a separate cell when the Surgeon is of opinion that it would be dangerous to his health or mind.' Those released would re-enter the world in their own clothes, and without the stigma of the shaved-head or close-cropped mop which might otherwise have marked him out as a former felon. Prisoners 'wishing advice on their discharge' were invited to 'state such a wish to the Governor, who will give full consideration to it, and act as he shall see best for the advantage of the prisoner.' It was a new world. Just how far this ideal of good practice was achieved may be put in question by the testimony of the prisoners themselves.

'There's nae luck about this house'

A peculiar insight into the life of prisoners living under this reformed regime is provided by a verse, *The Prison*, composed by James Nicol, confined – as 'Prisoner No.22' – to the County Jail in August 1867. It has a curiously affecting quality: the mantra of the first verse, a borrowed refrain from a popular eighteenth-century ballad, *There's Nae Luck About This House*, serving as a dismal chorus to all subsequent stanzas, and creating some sense of the weary drudge of daily life within this solitary domain:

There's nae luck about this house,
There's nae luck ava;
There's little pleasure in this house,
I wish I were awa.

Lock'd up like cattle, day and night,
And dine on cabbage leaves,
While round about in every cell
Are nought but rogues and thieves.

For forty days I've had to stay,
And twenty days I've more,
Before they let me out again,
And past that iron door.

Some picking oakum all the day,
Some plating ninesome ropes,

Some grinding on the heavy crank,
Some nursing future hopes.

The cell is small and dim and dark,
The window is so high,
When'er you try to look out through't
You see nought but the sky.

For bed you've got a wooden board,
A log fixed at the head;
For all the world like what is used
For stretching out the dead.

A stool is all the furniture
Within the darksome cell,
But it must hold your tin and spoon,
And soap and comb as well.

Speed on ye minutes, fly ye hours,
Till twenty days are o'er,
Then I may leave this dreary house,
And never see it more.

Cells on the ground floor of the prison, restored to their original condition in 1996 – replete with appropriate fixtures and fittings – are on daily display within the modern visitor attraction, the Stirling Old Town Jail, which occupies the site. They confirm Nicol's bleak picture of the bare room which, save for one equally solitary, silent and scrupulously supervised fifteen-minute exercise period on the roof walkway each day, would constitute his world for the duration of his sentence.

The food was poor. Prisoners *were* fed, something that had rarely been the case within the Tolbooth until its final two decades of service, and three meals a day were offered, but – despite the instructions of the County Prison Board that foodstuffs provided to prisoners 'must be of the best quality' – these were required to be 'even more monotonous than the…meagre dietary' previously provided. By Nicol's time the repast of most common prisoners consisted – as convict Frederick Brocklehurst (quoted in Philip Priestley's excellent *Victorian Prison Lives* (1999)) complained – of a weekly diet of 'seven pounds of brown-to-black bread and ten and a half pints of "stirabout". This latter item, known commonly as 'Skilly' (from the Irish *Skillagalee*), was a staple of prison fare: a watery oatmeal and barley broth or gruel to which bread, potatoes and meat – 'horse-meat, I'd wager', in the estimation of

Doune felon Alastair Thom, imprisoned for theft in the 1870s – might be added. This (largely liquid) diet was supplemented, in rather more tasteful fashion, with cocoa, flavoured with skimmed milk and molasses. Nicol's claim to 'dine on cabbage leaves' may simply be a rare example of *poetic license*: the fare offered by most penitentiaries of this era was intentionally bland and monotonous, but only *rarely* extended to the provision of fresh green vegetables. The nutritious diet promised by the County Prison Board was anything but: prisoners were often malnourished, and cases of scurvy were not uncommon.

As with the workhouse, picking oakum was a regular occupation, with convicts often required to strip up to 2lb of caulking material in a single day. An onerous labour, this at least gave prisoners some sense of purpose – something which could not be said for those poor souls set to 'grinding on the heavy crank'. The Crank – Appold's self-regulating hard labour machine – was pointless by design: an instrument of repetitive and meaningless toil, described by Major Arthur Griffiths during an 1872 visit to London's Millbank prison as 'a wheel set against cogs that exercised a resisting pressure, and turned by a handle weighted at will to fix the amount of effort required to make the revolution'. By tightening the gears wardens

Crank machine: the rusted remains of an original crank, from the old County Jail. An instrument of 'repetitive and meaningless labour', it served only to exhaust and break the spirit of those forced to use it. (Photo by David Kinnaird, courtesy of Stirling District Tourism)

could increase internal resistance and, correspondingly, the effort required of the prisoner to turn the crank-handle. As few as 100 or as many as 14,400 revolutions might be demanded, daily, often performed, as Alastair Thom complained, when assigned a one-thousand turns on the crank (for speaking to another prisoner), 'with one good arm bound behind my back'. The rusted, wall-mounted shell of a Crank mounted on the wall of one cell which had not been restored in the Old Town Jail shows a dial which would have displayed a countdown of the required revolutions. Hinges show this to have been covered, preventing the inmate from keeping track of his toil. Fearful of the consequences of failing to meet the warden's demands, he might easily be left to persist in his efforts long after he had fulfilled his obligations. Aside from the humiliation and despair of, as Major Griffiths put it, 'labouring hard to achieve no sort of result', the Crank was often the cause of lasting physical harm: Thom was, by his own account, 'like as a cripple for many months to come'. Mercifully those interred in the County Jail were spared that most terrible of Victorian penal punishments, the Treadwheel – a type of mill operated by a moving walkway, the prisoner effecting the rotation of the interior mechanism by forcing his full weight down on the steps. A day's toil might be set at as much as three miles – each tread on the Wheel constituting one foot. Dr John Mason Good, physician to Coldbath Fields penitentiary, Middlesex, warned in the 1870s of the 'strain or morbid exertion which it perpetually endangers by its peculiar effects on the muscles and other organs of the loins and abdominal region'. It is thought that regular punishment on the Wheel contributed

Food for thought: as plans for the new County Jail proceeded, Stirling's prisoners were finally fed. The 'best quality' fare promised often did not live up to expectations. (Author's collection)

STIRLING PRISON.

TENDERS WANTED for the Supply of the following Articles, for the Use of the Prison at Stirling, for Three Months, commencing on the 29th day of October curt., and to be delivered at the Prison weekly, or at such other times, and in such quantities, as may be required, viz.:—Oatmeal, per boll of 140 lbs.; Necks of Beef, per lb; Barley and Pease, mixed, per lb.; Split Peas, per lb.; Brosemeal, per stone; Bread, in coarse Rolls or Baps, 4 oz. each, per dozen; Butter Milk and Skim Milk, per imperial gallon; Salt, per cwt.; Pepper, Soda, Black and Brown Soap, per lb.; Pipeclay, Oat Straw, and Coals, per cwt.; Potatoes, per peck of 14 lbs.; Salt Herrings, per barrel, containing 1000 or 1200; and Treacle, per lb. The whole articles must be of the best quality; and further particulars will be learned on application to ROBERT CAMPBELL, Writer in Stirling, Clerk to the County Prison Board, with whom offers must be lodged on or before MONDAY the 28th instant.

Stirling, 23d October, 1844.

Still in use: a free-standing crank machine in the Old Town Jail Visitor Attraction. Visitors can test their endurance on this once-feared instrument of needless toil. (Photo by David Kinnaird, courtesy of Stirling District Tourism)

Cells were simply set out, with four bare white walls, a hammock and a wash basin. Under the Separate System, prisoners were allowed out of their cells for only 15 minutes exercise each day. (Picture by David Kinnaird, courtesy of Stirling District Tourism) to the rapid physical decline and early death of the poet Oscar Wilde, so soon after his release from Reading Jail, in 1897. By this time this foul device had been absent from Scots prisons for four decades. 'It was…with much satisfaction', wrote Frederick Hill in *An Autobiography of Fifty Years* (1896), 'that soon after entering on my official work I saw the last treadmill banished from Scotland.'

Paid work *was* available, (though offering as little as a penny a day, in some cases, such as the County Jail, noted in 1854), both Hill and Brebner being convinced that meagre reward in return for honest hard work was a necessary tool of reform. Stirling's new jail offered limited vocational training in net-making, hand-loom weaving and cobbling – all creating revenue for the jail. Such toil was reserved solely for male prisoners. Female inmates, incarcerated on the ground floor and isolated from any male contact, were assigned domestic duties by the Matron: work deemed appropriate to their sex and class. Those (male prisoners, again) unable to read or write were tutored by their jailors, and encouraged to study and reflect on scripture.

Initially hammocks, hooked to the walls, were provided for sleeping, rather than the 'wooden board' our poet describes. These could be rolled up and shelved at the start of the day, creating a large open workspace for the day's labours. After early success, expense caused grudging public support for the reformed experiment to waver. Rehabilitation was again sidelined by parsimony. The Reverend Sidney Smith, in 1822, defined the successful prison as a 'terror to evil-doers'. By the time of James Nicol's imprisonment, Stirling's County Jail was run along the lines proposed by that uncharitable clergyman: 'there must be a great deal of solitude; coarse food; a dress of shame; hard, incessant, irksome eternal labour; a planned and regulated and unrelenting exclusion of happiness and comfort.' In the 1860s, as overcrowding again became an issue, any attempt at the rehabilitation or reform of the individual offender was forgotten: jailors became little more than turnkeys, once more.

In 1888, despite local protests and questions raised in the House of Lords by the Earl of Mar, Stirling was to lose its county jail – after only forty-one years of service. Subject to a compulsory purchase order by the Crown, it became Scotland's only military detention barracks, remaining in use in that capacity until 1935, before beginning a slow decline into dereliction not remedied until renovations in the early 1990s. Stirling's prisoners were to be briefly confined once more within the neglected cells of the Tolbooth, but within a few years the Burgh was to have no jail at all – those convicted by its courts being summarily despatched to Glasgow or Perth.

Greater reforms were to come. Cornton Vale Garden Colony, established in 1907, did not admit 'Prisoners or Paupers', but offered first-time offenders and those on probation a harsh but disciplined introduction to market gardening and a *possibility* of escape from what must once have seemed an endless cycle of

Short sharp stock: Warden Hislop (author David Kinnaird) explains the rules and regulations of the reformed County Jail during live tours of the Stirling Old Town Jail. (Picture courtesy of Stirling District Tourism)

The Stirling Old Town jail is open to the public from Easter until Halloween each year.

desperation, dependency and crime. Such institutions represented an emerging awareness that the prevention of crime and criminality was a fundamentally *social* issue most effectively addressed by willing, compassionate communities. It had been more than a century since the Town Wall had been torn down, but Stirling's insular sensibility had been slow to dissipate. Now the same worthies who had once urged their Bailies to put vagrants and vagabonds out of sight and mind, were gradually acknowledging that this outlook actually perpetuated the cycles of criminality and social resentment which had filled the Burgh's cells and courtrooms for generations. As a boys' Borstal (from 1946) and women's prison (since 1975) Cornton Vale has not been without its critics, and it is far from the perfect penitentiary Howard dreamed of, even now, but it is hard to believe that he – along with Brebner, Hill and those other early reformers – would not approve the efforts of successive generations of governors, guards and administrators in moving toward that vital understanding that punishment is only part of the solution they so desperately sought to the 'problem of crime'.

Stirling's willingness to acknowledge just how far it has come from the barbarity of earlier eras is best exemplified by the Stirling Old Town Jail, based within the *new* County Jail. Since 1996, tourists and locals have been entertained and enlightened by Hangman Jock Rankin, reformer Frederick Hill and a host of prisoners, matrons and warders drawn from the Old Town's rich and colourful history of crime and punishment – brought vividly to life through comedy, drama and audience participation by actors from the Heritage Events Company – and offering, still, a sage warning to prospective evildoers as to the consequences of their wicked ways.

AFTERWORD

This book has, in part at least, looked at how a few brave souls have looked at the injustice of society and sought means to better the lot not merely of the majority of the population, but the individual too. Brebner, Hill and Howard are genuinely inspirational figures. What made them remarkable was not their exceptional energy or commitment, but their simple belief that they should do as they did because it was the right thing to do. Such inspirations are, and should be, commonplace: we just have to look for them.

As I completed my first book for The History Press, *Haunted Stirling*, in Spring 2010, the daughter of some dear friends died, just a few days short of her sixteenth birthday. She was the victim of Turner's Syndrome, a rare chromosomal disorder typified by cytogenetic abnormalities, which affects around one in two thousand women, increasing their susceptibility to ovarian cancer.

Eilidh Brown was an astonishing young lady – no, let me correct that – Eilidh Brown *is* an astonishing young lady. Over the last year of her life she endured hours of chemotherapy and hair loss, and physical pain and indignities I cannot hope to comprehend. But for all the misery life threw at her, despite the injustice and sheer bloody unfairness of her fate, she fought on. When her life-span was calculated in *days*, she wrestled them into *months*. When the comforting oblivion of unconsciousness beckoned, she dug in her heels, determined not to (as some hack or other put it) 'go easy into that good night'. She knew death was inevitable, but, for all her fear (and, who wouldn't be afraid, least of all a child?), she remained positive, giving her family and friends faith in the possibility of hope, and the strength to face her ultimate fate. This remarkable girl showed greater forbearance in the face of her own mortality than most adults I know. I wouldn't be so brave, I'm sure of that.

She passed away on 25 March 2010 – but hasn't stopped fighting. Her legacy, the Eilidh Brown Trust, was set up in the hope of establishing a cottage – not a hospice or a hospital, but a place where the families of children similarly afflicted can spend time together – a temporary refuge from the stresses illness places upon them, in the picturesque backdrop of modern Stirling. As I write this, the Trust is on the verge of achieving charitable status.

I dedicated *Haunted Stirling* to Eilidh, and urged its readers to visit the Trust's website (www.eilidhbrown.co.uk). Not enough. Not by a long shot. Inspired by the example of Eilidh's mother and father, Nicole and Gordon, and the many talented performers – including actor Billy Boyd, The Fratellis and stars of TV shows such as *River City* and *Still Game* – who freely gave of their time and energy at 'A Concert For the Love of Eilidh' at Stirling's MacRoberts Theatre on 15 January 2011, I have decided that any profits I might receive from sales of this book should go to Eilidh's cause. Thank you, then, for buying *Auld Stirling Punishments*. Every little helps.

If the example of the reformers teaches us anything, it is the truth of John Donne's adage that, 'No man is an island entire of itself; every man is a piece of the continent, a part of the main', and that's as true now as it was in 1624.

David Kinnaird

BIBLIOGRAPHY

Books

Black, George F. (Ed.), *Calendar of Cases of Witchcraft in Scotland, 1510-1727* (Kessinger Publishing, Whitefish, 2003)

Brammeld, Marie, *The Vagabond Book of Stirling: 1752-1787* (Lomax Press, Stirling, July 2010)

Bruce, Lady Martha; Hills, Charles; Murphy, John & Poor, Dick *A Century of Corntonvale* (The Smith Art Gallery & Museum, Stirling, 2010)

Cook, W.B., *Notes for a New History of Stirling* (Transactions of the Stirling Natural History Society, Stirling, 1898-1899)

Drysdale, William, *Old Biggins of Stirling: Its Closes, Wynds & Neebour Villages* (Eneas MacKay, Stirling, 1904)

Drysdale, William, *Old Faces, Old Places and Old Stories of Stirling* (Eneas MacKay, Stirling, 1898)

Evans, E.P., *The Criminal Prosecution and Capital Punishment of Animals* (Heineman, London, 1906)

Fleming, J.S., *The Old Ludgings of Stirling* (Eneas MacKay, Stirling, 1897)

Fleming, J.S., *Old Nooks of Stirling* (Eneas MacKay, Stirling, 1898)

Green, C.J., *Trials for High Treason in Scotland* (James Ballantyne & Co, Edinburgh, 1825)

Harrison, John G., *The Stirling Tolbooth: The Building and the People* (report for Scottish Development Agency, 1989)

Harrison, John G., *The World of John Cowane* (Report for Stirling District Council, 1989)

Hill, Frederick, *An Autobiography of Fifty Years* (E. Bentley & Son, London, 1896)

Hill, Frederick, *Crime: Its Amount, Causes and Remedies* (John Murray, London, 1853)

Holder, Geoff, *The Guide to Mysterious Stirlingshire* (The History Press, Stroud, 2008)

Howard, John, *The State of Prisons in England and Wales* (William Eyres, London, 1777)

Keay, John & Julia *Collins, Encyclopaedia of Scotland* 2nd Ed. (Collins, London, 2000)

Kinnaird, David, *Haunted Stirling* (The History Press, Stroud, 2010)

Mair, Craig, *Stirling: The Royal Burgh* (John Donald, Edinburgh, 1990)

Mair, Craig, *Alan Mair: Last Man Hanged in Stirling* (Stirling District Libraries, 1993)

Priestly, Philip, *Victorian Prison Lives* (Pimlico, London, 1999)

Renwick, Robert (Ed.), *Extracts from the Records of the Royal Burgh of Stirling,* AD *1471-1752* (Glasgow and Stirlingshire Sons of the Rock Society, Glasgow, 1889)

Ronald, James, *Landmarks of Old Stirling* (Eneas MacKay, Stirling, 1899)

Small, John W., *The Ludgings of the Earl of Mar* (Eneas MacKay, Stirling, 1905)

Young, Alex F., *Encyclopaedia of Scottish Executions: 1750-1963* (Eric Dobby Publishing, Kent, 1998)

Other

Broadsides for the executions of John Baird & Andrew Hardie, John Campbell, Alan Mair, William Taylor, and Janet M'Dougall (National Library of Scotland)

Other titles published by The History Press

Haunted Stirling

DAVID KINNAIRD

Drawing on historical and contemporary sources, this selection includes strange happenings from the Old Town, the Tolbooth, Argyll's Lodging, Mars Walk, Church of the Holy Rude and Thistles Shopping Centre, among many others. From sinister footsteps in the Governor's Block to the Green Lady of Stirling Castle, a phantom attired in Highland dress to eyewitness reports of poltergeist activity, *Haunted Stirling* is guaranteed to intrigue both believers and skeptics alike.

978 0 7524 5844 1

A History of Stirling in 100 Objects

ELSPETH KING

A History of the World in 100 Objects by the British Museum and the BBC is a project which has fired the public imagination throughout the land. *A History of Stirling in 100 Objects* is the first published tribute act. Compiled by Elspeth King and with photography by Michael McGinnes, collections curator, this book features 100 objects — all from the collections of the Stirling Smith Art Gallery and Museum — that each show a different aspect of Stirling's history.

978 0 7524 5932 5

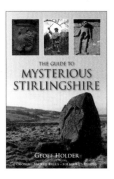

The Guide to Mysterious Stirlingshire

GEOFF HOLDER

This is a comprehensive guide to the county' ancient sites and archaeological curiosities, from tourist attractions such as Stirling Castle and Dunblane Cathedral to strange carvings, stone circles, and hidden cairns. With countless tales of encounters with ghosts, magical beings and monsters, a full list of all Stirlingshire's witch trials and the real story of Robert Kirk, the 'Fairy Minister', who is reputed to have been abducted by the Little Folk in the seventeenth century, this fascinating addition to Geoff Holder's best-selling series will delight residents, walkers and tourists alike.

978-0-7524-4768-1

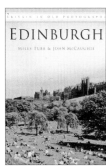

Edinburgh in Old Photographs

MILES TUBB & JOHN MCCAUGHIE

This fascinating selection of 170 archive images, each with a detailed caption, captures some of the changes and developments that have taken place in Edinburgh between the 1850s and 1970s. This book will appeal to everyone with an interest in the history of Edinburgh, and will awaken memories of days gone by for all who know and love this beautiful part of Scotland.

978 0 7524 5918 9

Visit our website and discover thousands of other History Press books.

www.thehistorypress.co.uk